I make peo~~ple~~ ...

–Jesus to Matthew

Never been to a wedding banquet but I'm on my way to one.

–John the Baptist to his executioners, Episode #1

We worship a living God, and you are his son.

–Peter to Jesus, Episode #2

He put mud on my eyes, and I wash, and I see.

–Blind man to the Pharisees, Episode #3

We are in mourning with you. We grieve.

–Jesus to Kafni, Episode #4

My son is as good as healed. Let's go.

–Gaius to Peter and Matthew, Episode #4

Mary has chosen to feast on something of eternal value.

–Jesus to Martha, Episode #5

I've done the math, and it does not add up.

–Matthew to Judas, Episode #6

I'm trying not to be angry. You didn't come sooner, Lord.

–Martha to Jesus, Episode #7

I've seen some things that I can't explain.

–Atticus to Pontius Pilate, Episode #8

The Chosen Study Library

For: skeptics... observers... seekers... learners... followers.

THE CHOSEN STUDY
10 Studies from 8 Episodes in Each Guide

Season 1	Season 2	Season 3	Season 4	Season 5	Season 6	Season 7

WATER	HOPE	FOOD	SIGHT			

THE BIBLE IN THE CHOSEN
20 Studies from 20 Scenes in Each Guide

Season 1	Season 2	Season 3	Season 4	Season 5	Season 6	Season 7

Find the (eventual) 140 YouTube Chosen Scene Playlist at:
tinyurl.com/chosen-playlist-1 (others: -2, -3, -4, -5, -6, -7)

The Chosen Study
SIGHT FOR THE BLIND

The Chosen Study
SIGHT FOR THE BLIND

A welcoming and
Interactive experience for everyone:
skeptics... observers... seekers... learners... followers.

The Jesus Study Team

Bill & Teresa Syrios, Dietrich Gruen,
Dave Hawkins, Mark Syrios, and Don & Cathy Baker

The CHOSEN SERIES

*Watch > Discover > Relate
the Most Audacious
Story ever told.*

The FOURTH SEASON

*I am the light of the world. Whoever follows me
will not walk in darkness, but will have the light of life.*
-John 8:12

Crossover Press

©2024 *Sight for the Blind: The Chosen Study, Season Four*
(Ten Studies Inspired by The Chosen)
Bill Syrios & TJS Team

Scripture quotations are from the ESV® Bible (The Holy Bible, English Standard Version®), ©2001 by Crossway, a publishing ministry of Good News Publishers. The cover art is from ©Melani Pyke: melanipyke.com. Used by permission.

The Jesus Study and their guides are not affiliated
with *The Chosen* TV show or *the Come and See Foundation*.

ISBN: 979-8-9875774-1-7

"**The Chosen** is a television drama based on the life of Jesus Christ, created, directed and co-written by American filmmaker, Dallas Jenkins. It is the first multi-season series about the life of Christ, and season one was the highest crowd-funded TV series or film project of all time.

The series' creators stated that they had hoped to distinguish the new series from previous portrayals of Jesus by crafting a multi-season, episode-based story. The series portrays Jesus 'through the eyes of those who met him.'" —*The Chosen*, Wikipedia

The Chosen Study focuses on *filling out* the series with Scripture passages to take everyone deeper. The guide can profitably be used by individuals with the hope that they... we... facilitate outreach and learning with others in one-on-one and group contexts. After all: *People must know!*

Contents

Welcome to The Chosen Study, Season Four 8

Study and Discussion Format 9

A Word as We Begin 13

Studies, Discussions, Teachings

Study #1: Promises, Episode 1 17
   Luke 1:5-16, 39-45; Mark 6:14-29

Study #2: Confessions, Part 1, Episode 2A and 2B 31
   Matthew 10:34-39; Matthew 16:13-20

Study #3: Confessions, Part 2, Episode 2C 51
   Matthew 5:21-48, 38-48; Matthew 18: 15-35

Study #4: Moon to Blood, Episode 3 63
   John 9:1-6, 13-34; Matthew 23:1-17, 23-31

Study #5: Calm Before, Episode 4 77
   Matthew 8:5-13; Mark 10:38-42

Study #6: Sitting, Serving, Scheming, Episode 5 89
   Mark 7:1-12; Luke 10::21-43

Study #7: Dedication, Episode 6 103
   John 10:1-20; 10:22-39

Study #8: The Last Sign, Episode 7 119
   John 11:17-44; Isaiah 53:1-6

Study #9: Humble, Episode 8A, 8B and 8C 133
   Ex. 12:1-14; John 11:45-57: Matt. 25:31-45; Micah 6:6-8

Study #10: Humble, Part 2, Episode 8A, 8B, and 8C 149
   John 12:1-8; Mark 11:1-7; John 6:63-68

Your Faith Journey 161

Background Notes 169

Leader's Notes 181

Study and Leadership Resources 191

Welcome to The Chosen Study, Season Four

The English word "gospel" comes from the Greek term, *evangelion*, which means "good news." The four gospel (good news) writers wanted their readers to not only know how remarkable Jesus was, but to know how good his message becomes in the lives of those who embrace it.

To understand their message better, we watch, study, and discuss Chosen episodes with complementary biblical passages. So, wherever you may be spiritually—**skeptic... observer... seeker... learner... or follower**—we're glad you've joined in to learn from those who knew Jesus best.

Flexible Time Options: Food + Film + Scripture + Discussion

Longer: WATCH > DISCOVER > RELATE with food, as set out in this guide, takes *2½ to 3 hours*. **This format is most impactful and cited below.** *

Medium: If limited to *1½ to 2 hours*, you will need to skip questions or eliminate a "Discover" section to condense and keep up the pace.

Shorter: If the group has less time, say *an hour*, you could: 1) watch the episode, and 2) study the passages before coming. Then as you meet, you would discuss what you watched and studied in preparation. is less than ideal if members' preparation is inconsistent.)

*EXAMPLE: Midweek or Sunday	*EXAMPLE: Saturday Morning
5:45 ARRIVE: 15 min. to gather	**8:45 ARRIVE:** 15 min. to gather
6:00 POTLUCK: 30 min. relax/eat	**9:00 LITE BREAKFAST:** 30 min.
6:30-8:30 THE CHOSEN STUDY	**9:30-11:30 THE CHOSEN STUDY**

OFFICIAL TRAILER 2:31

Invite Others to Join

Email or text the **2:30 min. trailer** to those interested in coming to your group (also see pages 181-188): tinyurl.com/trailer-season-four

NOTE FOR EVERYONE: We use **"tinyurl.com"** to create shortened URLs for you to type into your browser window to access most of the videos.

GUIDE OVERVIEW: 3-Step Process ➞ Drive it Home

The Chosen Study guide provides a means of bringing people together to study and discuss Chosen episodes with Scripture. This framework gives direction to dynamic group studies and discussions:

PRIOR To STUDY

How to Lead the Study

Tips to help current (and future) leaders prepare. Please read page 16 carefully.

1 **WATCH** View Episode Together > Discuss — **FROM The CHOSEN**

Questions that take us deeper into the episode.

2 **DISCOVER** Read Passage > Mark It Up > Discuss — **FROM The BIBLE**

Intro, "Look Fors," Questions to grasp meaning.

3 **RELATE** Apply Insights to God, Life, and Yourself > Discuss

Questions that help us apply the passage in our lives.

T-Shirt Design Create a memorable one-liner

Crystallize your thoughts in a slogan or drawing.

GUIDE COMMENTARY & ARTISTIC LICENSE

Notes on the Study Commentary and Historical Context

The biblical passages' context and meaning put into perspective.

REALISTIC But REAL? That's plausible but did it happen?

The Chosen's artistic license put into perspective.

PERSONAL FOLLOW-UP AFTER YOUR GROUP STUDY

Drive it Home ... **Video Insights** ... **Worship—Pray—Share**

A. C. T. S Prayer: Adoration/Confession/Thanksgiving/Supplication

1) WATCH View Episode 1 Together (52 min.) > Discuss

Example, Season Four, Episode 1:

On next page

Promises

Luke 1:5-8; 11-17: 39-45; Mark 6:14-29

2) DISCOVER Read Text > Mark It Up > Discuss

General Example, The Word Became Flesh: John 1:1–14

Ask the "W" Questions

WHO is involved | **WHEN** did it happen | **WHERE** is it happening
WHAT is taking place | **HOW** is it happening... and then ask...
WHY questions to uncover the author's original meaning.

*The *"Look For"* at the end of each **INTRO** provides initial direction.

**Mark Up the passage(s) by using
a FOUR-COLORED BIC PEN to draw:**

On next page

Circles around people or places
Boxes around whatever you'd like
–Lines under key words and phrase
Clouds wherever you'd feel like it.
–Identify change of scene, watch for
contrast, repetition, key words

–Write notes in the margins

3) RELATE Apply to God & Life | After Study: Drive it Home

Express Your Thoughts:
Write, discuss, and live out applications from the passages in your life— your relationship with God, with others, your values, priorities, goals.

On page 12

How to WATCH The Chosen

Go to thechosen.tv and access each season under the "Watch" tab. You can also search for *The Chosen* in your phone's app store or stream it to your smart TV from The Chosen app, or from providers like Prime, Netflix or The CW.

The Chosen

Always **turn on the TV's closed captions** to better follow the narrative. **Darken the room** to better enhance the action. A big TV also helps!

Note: We identify the length of each episode (or segment of a episode) in the WATCH sections to help you pace the study.

Remember, it's better to leave things unsaid than to bog down.

How to DISCOVER a passage's meaning: Example

Similar to Genesis   *The Word predates Time as God*

John 1: In the beginning was the Word, and the Word was with God, and the Word was God. ² He was in the beginning with God. ³ All things were made through him, and without him was not any thing made that was made. ⁴ In him was life, and the life was the light of men. The light shines in the darkness, and the darkness has not overcome it. ⁶ There was

"A man" came as a witness to "the Word"/"the Light"
a man sent from God, whose name was John. ⁷ He came as a witness, to bear witness about the light, that all might believe through him. ⁸ He was not the light, but came to bear witness about the light.

⁹ The true light, which gives light to everyone, was coming into the
                                    Light to show the world
world. ¹⁰ He was in the world, and the world was made through him, yet not receive him. ¹² But to all who did receive him, who believed in his name, he gave the right to become children of God....

The results of believing and receiving = becoming

How to use the guide's questions: GENERAL then SPECIFIC

Unlike most Bible studies, these studies consider the fact that your group has just spent time studying (*Discover* section). So, instead of using the guide's questions first, **start with "general questions,"** like:

... Set the scene, who's involved, and what are they doing?

... What did you see (observe, notice, or appreciate) in this section?

... What strikes you (surprises you, or is something new to you) here?

Then, ask general follow-up questions like: *... Any other thoughts?*

Such questions often lead to an extended back-and-forth dialogue (see page 188). That's your discussion goal. If this happens, **you do not need to use many or any of the guide's more specific questions.** So, if or when the dialogue wanes or wanders from the main points, then you can use some of the guide's **more "specific questions,"** such as:

–How did John the Baptist prepare the way for Jesus?

–What did it mean when Peter called Jesus "the Christ"?

RELATE and T-Shirt Design for the passage's application

A few questions remain to help apply the text to your life and a T-Shirt Design for summarizing your most important takeaways (see page 23-24). Use these for a group wrap-up.

Drive it Home and Video Insights and Worship—Pray—Share

Schedule a quiet time during the week after the study—say on "your Sabbath"—to **review and respond** with *worship, prayer* and *sharing*.

The ***Drive it Home*** section continues with ***Video Insights***, which provide a variety of resources, from music videos to word studies to Bible teaching. This will expose you and your group to other growth opportunities. Next comes ***ACTS—Adoration, Confession, Thanksgiving, Supplication*** and *(Next) Steps* on page 29.

SIGHT FOR THE BLIND

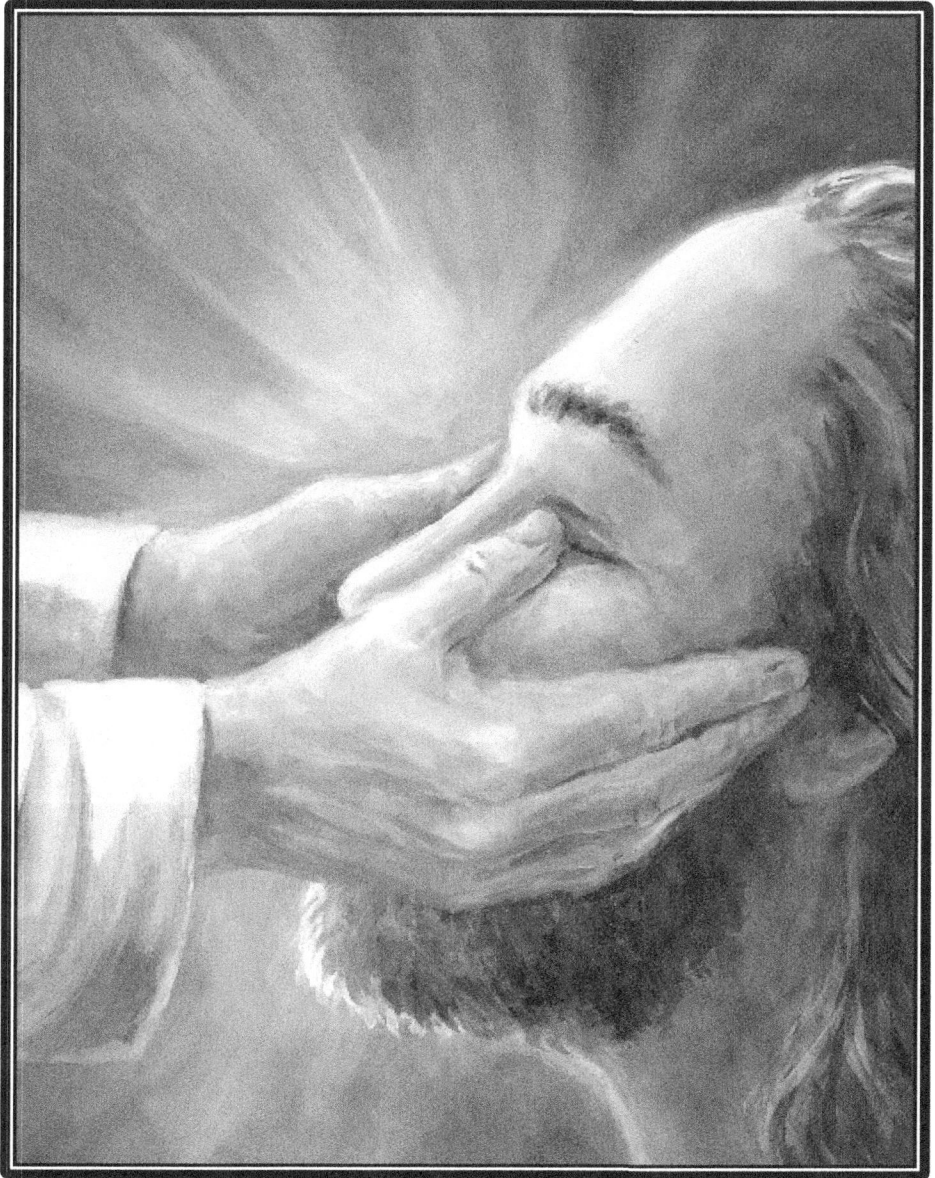

Some gain their sight, others don't. –John 9:1-41

A Word as We Begin

The Chosen is meant to take you into the eyes and ears of the people who followed Jesus. We believe that if you can see Jesus through the eyes of those who met him, you can be changed and impacted in the same way they were. If we can connect you with their burdens and struggles and questions, then ideally, we can connect you to the solution, to the answer to those questions.   –Dallas Jenkins

| One-on-One Get-Togethers | or | Small Group Meetings | or | Small/Large (8+) Group Gatherings |

The Chosen Study supports these aspirations by pairing The Chosen with Old and New Testament passages to take us deeper—together.
                    –The Jesus Study Team

PRIOR to STUDY

A preparation template for leading each study.

NOTE FOR LEADERS: Buy guides and four-colored BIC pens in advance. Participants can buy guides themselves, but it's often easier if one person buys them (from Amazon is easiest) along with (our suggestion) four-color BIC pens (find 6 or 12 BIC pen packs on Amazon). See guides at: jesusstudy.org/order-guides.

–**Exchange names** and personal info. Put together a sign-up sheet. (See page 188-189, or on the website under *Resources*.) Also have members **put their names on the back cover** for quick identification.

–**Watch part of the Chosen episode.** In this case leave out a discussion. (After other times, there will be time for discussion after the episode.)

–**Talk through the study format** by going through pages 9 to 11 so that everyone understands it right before you study Luke 1.

–**Have yourself or a prepared volunteer read aloud** the INTRO and LOOK FOR sections, then the Luke 1 passage (page 18-19).

–**Give members time for personal study** (ideally using four-color BIC pens). Answer questions on pages 19-20 as helpful. Monitor the time. Tell your group on which question to end, so they know how far to go.

–**Spend time reflecting on and designing your T-Shirt** as a summary of the episode or passage (pages 23-24). Then share these in the group.

–**Point out the *Notes* and *Realistic But Real* sections** after each study (pages 25-27). These sections are for reference, not for discussion.

–**Identify the *Drive it Home* and *Video Insights*** (pages 27-29) segments for your group. Encourage a midweek (or Sabbath) review.

–**Keep up the pace!** Time can pass more quickly than you expect, so watch the clock, leave things unsaid, and keep moving to finish on time.

This page is a prep template. Follow a similar pattern for each study.

Promises *(Season Four, Episode 1)*

Study #1

FROM *The* **CHOSEN**

BACKGROUND: In Season Four, opposition to Jesus steadily increases. Not only is Jesus hated, but so are those close to him. John the Baptist, who paved the way for Jesus, pays the ultimate price when he is beheaded. None of this takes Jesus by surprise; it is all part of the plan of salvation.

WATCH View Episode 1 (4 ½ min., from :20 to 4:43)

INTRO: John the Baptist is one of the most colorful characters in the New Testament, and in *The Chosen* as well. Even when he is not on the screen, he is frequently present in the minds and conversations of his former students and Jesus. This episode will focus on his story.

DISCOVER Read Aloud > Mark It Up > Discuss

INTRO: The lives of John the Baptist and Jesus were intertwined even before they were born. Luke 1 tells us that both of their births were foretold by angels, and recounts what happened when their mothers got together.

FROM The BIBLE

Look for prophesies concerning John, Jesus, and their mothers.

Birth of John the Baptist Foretold
LUKE 1 [5] In the days of Herod, king of Judea, there was a priest named Zechariah, of the division of Abijah. And he had a wife from the daughters of Aaron, and her name was Elizabeth. [6] And they were both righteous before God, walking blamelessly in all the commandments and statutes of the Lord. [7] But they had no child, because Elizabeth was barren, and both were advanced in years.

[8] Now while he was serving as priest before God . . . . [11] there appeared to him an angel of the Lord standing on the right side of the altar of incense. [12] And Zechariah was troubled when he saw him, and fear fell upon him.

[13] But the angel said to him, "Do not be afraid, Zechariah, for your prayer has been heard, and your wife Elizabeth will bear you a son, and you shall call his name John. [14] And you will have joy and gladness, and many will rejoice at his birth, [15] for he will be great before the Lord and he will be filled with the Holy Spirit, even from his mother' womb.

¹⁶ And he will turn many of the children of Israel to the Lord their God, ¹⁷ and he will go before him in the spirit and power of Elijah, to turn the hearts of the fathers to the children, and the disobedient to the wisdom of the just, to make ready for the Lord a people prepared for the Lord." . . .

Mary Visits Elizabeth

³⁹ In those days Mary arose and went with haste into the hill country, to a town in Judah, ⁴⁰ and she entered the house of Zechariah and greeted Elizabeth.

⁴¹ And when Elizabeth heard the greeting of Mary, the baby leaped in her womb. And Elizabeth was filled with the Holy Spirit, ⁴² and she exclaimed with a loud cry, "Blessed are you among women, and blessed is the fruit of your womb! ⁴³ And why is this granted to me that the mother of my Lord should come to me? ⁴⁴ For behold, when the sound of your greeting came to my ears, the baby in my womb leaped for joy. ⁴⁵ And blessed is she who believed that there would be a fulfillment of what was spoken to her from the Lord."

1. *What did the angel tell Zechariah about the character of his son?*

... What did he say John would do?

... How would John's life affect others?

2. *How did Elizabeth encourage Mary?*

3. The Holy Spirit is mentioned prominently in verses 15 and 41. *What is his role?*

… What does this passage teach you about the Holy Spirit?

WATCH   View Episode 1 *(47 min., from 5:45 to 52:35)*

INTRO: As you watch the rest of this episode, be aware of people's reactions to John the Baptist.

FROM
The CHOSEN

DISCOVER Read > Mark > Discuss RELATE

INTRO: Mark 6 explains how and why John the Baptist was executed. ***Look for people's opinions about Jesus and John.***

FROM
The BIBLE

The Death of John the Baptist
MARK 6 **14** King Herod heard of it [Jesus' disciples teaching, healing and casting out demons], for Jesus' name had become known. Some said, "John the Baptist has been raised from the dead. That is why these miraculous powers are at work in him." **15** But others said, "He is Elijah." And others said, "He is a prophet, like one of the prophets of old."

16 But when Herod heard of it, he said, "John, whom I beheaded, has been raised." **17** For it was Herod who had sent and seized John and bound him in prison for the sake of Herodias, his brother Philip's wife, because he had married her. [18] For John had been saying to Herod, "It is not lawful for you to have your brother's wife." [19] And Herodias had a grudge against him and wanted to put him to death. But she could not, [20] for Herod feared John, knowing that he was a righteous and holy man, and he kept him safe. When he heard him, he was greatly perplexed and yet he heard him gladly.

[21] But an opportunity came when Herod on his birthday gave a banquet for his nobles and military commanders and the leading men of Galilee. [22] For when Herodias's daughter came in and danced, she pleased Herod and his guests.

And the king said to the girl, "Ask me for whatever you wish, and I will give it to you." [23] And he vowed to her, "Whatever you ask me, I will give you, up to half of my kingdom."

[24] And she went out and said to her mother, "For what should I ask?" And she said, "The head of John the Baptist." [25] And she came in immediately with haste to the king and asked, saying, "I want you to give me at once the head of John the Baptist on a platter."

[26] And the king was exceedingly sorry, but because of his oaths and his guests he did not want to break his word to her. [27] And immediately the king sent an executioner with orders to bring John's head. He went and beheaded him in prison [28] and brought his head on a platter and gave it to the girl, and the girl gave it to her mother.

[29] When his disciples heard of it, they came and took his body and laid it in a tomb.

5. *Why did Herod think that Jesus might be a resurrected John?*

... What does this fear reveal about Herod?

6. *Why did Herodias want to kill John?*

... What does her hatred reveal about her?

7. *How did John prepare the way for Jesus?*

... How does he help you to better understand the ministry of Jesus?

T-Shirt Design After watching > discovering > relating, What slogan would you write or draw on your T-Shirt?

NOTE FOR EVERYONE: End by completing designing your T-shirt. Then share them with your group. On page one under *"I make people What they aren't"* and below are some T-shirt sayings. Feel free to get more creative...or not with your design and share it!

Example concepts or quotations summarizing the film:

How does your righteousness compare with to the Pharisees?

Remember: Don't build your house on sandy land!

Jesus is the Rock that doesn't Roll.

OR

You could DRAW a picture that summarizes your thoughts.

T-Shirt Design After watching > discovering > relating,
What slogan would you write or draw on your T-Shirt?

Wrap up by sharing with your group.

Draft concepts or quotations for summarizing this study:

Final design:

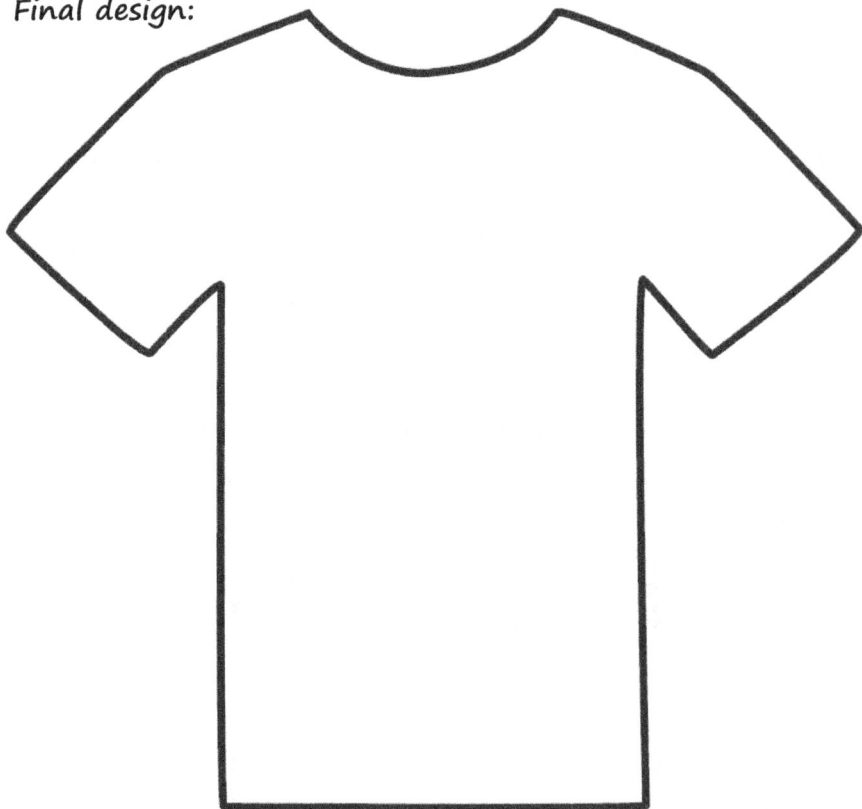

NOTE FOR EVERYONE: Don't be shy. Share what you created for your T-Shirt. Which other slogans or drawings do you particularly like from others in your group?

NOTES on Study #1 *Commentary and Historical Context*

Luke 1:5-8; 11-17—Birth of John the Baptist Foretold

- Zechariah belonged to Abijah, one of 24 divisions (I Chronicles 24:10) descended from Aaron. Abijah's clan, numbering 1000 priests by this time, took a week-long tour of temple duty every six months and "chosen by lot" to keep incense burning in front of the altar of the Most Holy Place continually.

- "No child" (v. 7) not only meant no personal disappointment but was seen as divine disfavor and social disgrace. God reversed this curse.

- Fear was a common reaction to angels (Judges 6:22-23; 13:22) as was angelic reassurance "Do not be afraid" (v. 13). Still unsure, Zechariah asked for a sign that he and Elizabeth, both up in years, would have a child. He is rebuked and rendered mute for this initial lack of faith. Joy replaces fear—a common theme in Luke (1:14,44,47,58; 2:10).

- Abstaining from alcoholic drinks typifies the ancient Nazirite vow (Numbers 6:1-4), as taken by the prophets Samson (Judges 13:4-7) and Samuel (1 Samuel 1:11), and now John the Baptist.

- John was a type of Elijah (Malachi 4:5-6). He typified a wilderness prophet paving the way for the Messiah as predicted by Isaiah (40:3-5).

Luke 1:39-45 — Mary Visits Elizabeth

- Mary journeys 80-100 miles to visit her aunt Elizabeth for support. The women rejoice in the exceptional miracles of their pregnancies.

Mark 6:14-29—The Death of John the Baptist

- Herod didn't realize that Jesus and John were contemporaries, or he would not be this confused about Jesus' identity. With an uneasy conscience for beheading John, Herod was also alarmed that John, in one form or another, had come back to haunt him. What follows is the backstory that details how John was killed in a power play.

- It was not lawful for a man to marry his brother's wife while that brother was still alive (Leviticus 18:16; 20:21). John called Herod to account for doing this wicked thing in marrying Herodias. She then avenged her shame by manipulating Herod to do her bidding in response to the lewd dance and bold request by Salome (the name of Herodias' daughter, according to Jewish historian Josephus).

REALISTIC But REAL?

That's plausible but did it happen?

Are the flashbacks of John's birth and life true? The storyline of the film follows the events of Scripture (Luke 1:5-25, 39-45) in retelling Mary's experience. Likewise, the events at Elizabeth's home—the unborn John leaping for joy, the muted Zechariah communicating that their child would be named John (not Zechariah)—unfolds much as in the account of Luke 1:57-66. After John's birth, Zechariah is moved to prophesy the work of John, just as recorded in Luke 1:67-79—a prophecy that came true even in leading to John's unjust but inevitable execution.

Was Joanna a secret disciple of John the Baptist and Jesus? Yes, a follower of Jesus (Luke 8:3; 24:10), but it's unknown whether she also followed John the Baptist. Likely John had a friendly advocate inside the Roman administration to facilitate visitors and messages to/from Jesus' followers and John in prison (7:18-23). Joanna was the wife of Chuza, Herod's household manager, so the Joanna-John connection is believable. This would have likely driven a wedge between her and her husband Chuza, as shown in the film.

Did Salome perform the perfect dance to get John beheaded? Perhaps the choreography is rooted in ancient (and lascivious) dancing rituals. Salome, who is Herodias' daughter and Herod Antipas' stepdaughter, has a dance instructor (which is plausible) who gets her ready to perform. her best-ever dance, as her scorned mother, Herodias, believes it would take a perfect performance for Herod to grant her wish. That wish is for the head of John the Baptist on a silver (wedding) platter which follows the account of Matthew 14:1-12 closely.

Did John the Baptist really make a statement about attending a wedding? No such statement is recorded in scripture, but *The Chosen* has included it to speak about the real marriage feast that is to come in Revelation 19:6-9. The imagery of this future wedding was also prophesied by Isaiah (54:5-7; 62:5) and Hosea (2:19-20). John used such wedding imagery in describing his ministry as that of an attendant in Jesus' wedding with his people (John 3:29). Therein, you will see that John the Baptist is holding onto the hope of the resurrection. The "lamb" (shown in the film) gives him peace to face a brutal execution.

Did John, James, and Zebedee strike it rich in the olive oil business? While the characters are real, their money-making business is fiction.

Was it really necessary to receive the father's blessing to marry in those days? Ramah, a fictional character introduced has been paired with Thomas ever since the Wedding at Cana (John 2:1-11), where they served wine together. She reports that her father Kafni (also fictional) is unwilling to bless their marriage. In situations where a man has violated an unengaged woman, the father has the right to intervene and halt a forced marriage (Exodus 22:16-17; Deuteronomy 22:28-29), thus stressing the importance of consent and protection for women. Ultimately, the decision to seek a father's blessing (and protection) is a cultural or personal choice—not a biblical mandate.

Drive it Home	Review and Respond: Worship, Pray, Share

John the Baptist's ministry was to introduce Jesus as *"the Lamb of God who takes away the sin of the world."* As a result of his testimony, the first disciples start following Jesus (John 1:29, 35)." Now, as he is about to be executed, in *The Chosen's* rendition, John sees the sky open and a lamb outside free to move around. In that moment he knows he has accomplished his role to "prepare the way" and is grateful for this magnificent confirmation.

Then, in Jesus' dream, John now unshackled, ushers him forth. John's death saddens Jesus but also provides the signal that all is ready for his coming with many more spiritually open. Normally we'd encourage you to sing along, but for this first song, you might just want to listen.

My King –CeCe Winans
Type in URL: tinyurl.com/my-king-song (4:11 min.)

Only Jesus –Casting Crowns
Type in URL: tinyurl.com/only-Jesus-song (3:49 min.)

10. *If you had lived in the time of John the Baptist, what would have attracted and/or repelled you about him*

11. *What events in your life have made you the most spiritually open?*

Video Insights 7 *Things you Didn't Know about John the Baptist*
Type in URL: <u>tinyurl.com/7-things-of-John</u> (24:31min.) –*Brandon Robbins*
Thoughts:
_____

The REAL Reason John the Baptist Was Killed –*Brandon Robbins*
Type in URL: <u>tinyurl.com/why-John-died</u> (31:10 min. – begin at 14:58)
Thoughts:
_____

The FIERY Message Of John The Baptist – *Rabbi Jason Sobel*
Type in URL: <u>tinyurl.com/fiery-message</u> (20:46 min. – begin at 7:15)
Thoughts:
_____

A. C. T. S. Prayer:
Adoration / Confession / Thanksgiving / Supplication / Steps

Examine where you are with the Lord and the priority of his kingdom. Take it to him in prayer:

ADORATION: How can you praise God from whom all blessings flow?

CONFESSION: What do you need to confess and change?

THANKSGIVING: Which circumstances will you thankfully embrace?

SUPPLICATION: For whom and for what will you pray?

Next STEPS: What will you do with what you've learned? With whom?

PRIOR to STUDY

Getting ready for the next study.

NOTE FOR LEADERS: Always begin by having new people introduce themselves.

NOTE FOR EVERYONE: This guide assumes no prior preparation, but there is a place for "post-study reflection" called:

Drive it Home

You have seen this for Study #1 on pages 27-29 and will see it for the next study on pages 47-49. Schedule a *God-encounter time* during the week to review and respond to your last study experience. We have included worship videos and questions to go deeper.

You also likely noted the section called:

Insight Videos

These videos are meant to give you a feel for the wide variety of available video resources. Such content provides more biblical insight and historical context to the passages being studied.

To access them, it is necessary to be precise when typing in their URL into your computer, tablet, or phone's browser window.

Finally, page 49 is for post-study prayer and "next steps" action:

A-C-T-S

Confessions (Episode 2A and 2B)

Study #2

FROM *The* **CHOSEN**

REVIEW: Take a few minutes to skim the events and characters in Seasons One, Two and Three on pages 32-37. Then answer and discuss the question on the top of page 38.

If you haven't yet seen these seasons, feel free to binge-watch them later!

Looking Back on Season One

Pilot Episode: The series opens with Jesus' birth story as experienced by **shepherds**, one of whom was lame. Having heard of Old Testament pro-phecies and having seen angels, they visit **Mary**, **Joseph**, and **baby Jesus**. Beholding the scene, they are transformed, even healed. They tell others, in Bethlehem and beyond, of the angels' proclamation—*the good news of great joy that will be for all the people* (Luke 2:10).

Episode One: The opening scene depicts a woman ("Lilith") in distress and demon-possessed. **Nicodemus,** a Pharisee from Jerusalem, is compelled by the Romans to exorcise her demons, but fails, causing him to question his faith. After a near-suicide attempt, Lilith meets Jesus, who calls her by her real name, **Mary of Magdala**. We also meet brothers, **Simon** and **Andrew**, fishermen with tax debts, and their tax collector, **Matthew,** all of whose lives are about to change.

Episode Two: To the distress of his overseer, **Gaius**, an earnest Matthew seeks out Roman praetor, **Quintus,** for help. Quintus ends up enlisting his help to catch fishermen who evade taxes on Shabbat (Sabbath). Nicodemus tracks down Mary to clarify the source of her demonic deliverance. Preparation for the Shabbat meal is made and celebrated by Jewish leaders, fishermen, Matthew with his dog, and Mary Magdalene. Mary hosts a meal for a small group, with the last arrival introduced as "the man who helped me."

Episode Three: Aptly titled, *Jesus Loves the Little Children*, the children are commended as examples for Jesus' students. All such students should listen to him and tell others about him. Through the eyes of **Abigail, Joshua "the Brave,"** and the other children, we see how kind and purposeful Jesus is. Our challenge: Embrace such a childlike faith!

Episode Four: The series pivots from Jesus with children to a defining moment in his childhood when he spent three days at the temple, unbeknownst to his parents. When they found him, Jesus asks, *"Didn't you know I must be in my Father's House?"* Twenty years later, Jesus and his students attend a wedding at Cana. While there, he confounds everyone—the wedding party, wine stewards, **Ramah** and **Thomas**, as well as his students—by turning water into wine. This miracle remedies the crisis at hand. This "sign" also answers his mother's challenge, *"If not now, when?"* Jesus' intervention reveals more of who he is and about his mission. Later, Nicodemus questions **John the Baptist** in prison, eager to learn more regarding the coming Messiah.

Episode Five: The fishermen have failed in their efforts to pay back taxes to Rome. Roman officials are not to be trifled with and Simon faces the imminent consequence of imprisonment or worse. Only a miracle can save him and that, surprisingly, is what happens. The huge catch leads Simon to repentance and faith. Jesus promises to turn fishermen into fishers of people. Simon then communicates his new vocation to his wife, Eden. She enthusiastically supports this change, telling him: *"Someone finally sees in you what I have always seen. You're more than a fisherman."*

Episode Six: Jesus' compassion is on full display. He heals a leper and a paralytic, showcasing the faith of their friends. As Jesus' followers witness his care, their faith in him grows, as does the resistance among religious leaders who consider his claims and actions blasphemous. Some are jealous, while others are intrigued, as they sort out what to make of this itinerant miracle worker from Nazareth.

Episode Seven: Building common ground with Nicodemus, Jesus takes us back to Moses and the bronze serpent, which was lifted up in the wilderness, and healed God's people by faith. He calls unlikely converts to *"follow me."* Matthew is called and follows immediately—much to the consternation of Simon. Jesus' disciples are divided by personal, political, and even ethnic points of views. Jesus urges Simon (and us) to: *"Get used to different!"*

Episode Eight: The final episode begins with a flashback to Jacob's Well. This sets up the following scene where Jesus and his students head straight through the hated and dangerous region of Samaria. Jesus stops at Jacob's Well where he meets **Photina**, an outcast woman of Samaria. Their encounter reveals the life and mission of Jesus and his disciples, as we will soon see in Season Two.

Looking Back on Season Two

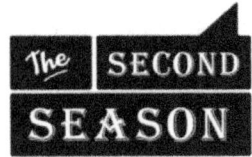

Episode 1: The opening scene not only sets the stage for Season Two, but it also serves as prologue for how the Gospels were written. Here we find **John** interviewing witnesses, writing notes, and musing with Jesus' mother, Mary, about how to begin his Gospel.

After Jesus encounters **Photina** (the Samaritan woman), he and his disciples visit her hometown of Sychar for two days (John 4:43). During this time, **James** and **John** till a field, and the disciples "lose" Jesus while he fixes a cart axle. Also, Photina's husband, among others, listens to Jesus tell the Parable of the Lost Sheep (Luke 15:1-7). The parable foreshadows a fascinating encounter with a "lost sheep" (**Melech)** and is an interesting reference to the Good Samaritan parable.

Episode 2: The disciples welcome **Philip**—a student of John the Baptist, and friend of Andrew. Now changing allegiance from John to Jesus, he seeks out his old friend, **Nathanael,** with whom he shares the good news. Nathanael (in this show, a failed architect) was despondent over a collapsed building and the loss of his career. But he finds new purpose in meeting and following the man who *saw* him under a fig tree.

Episode 3: No new characters, but crowds of people line up for healing. We listen in on compelling insights as the disciples, including Jesus' mother, Mary, seek to understand the movement they have joined. Tensions rise as Simon and Andrew confront Matthew about his former life. But their arguments look petty as an exhausted Jesus returns, laboring as he walks through the camp to his tent.

Episode 4: Here we meet **Jesse**, permanently lame from a childhood accident, until he is healed by Jesus some 38 years later (John 5:1-9). His brother in this show, **Simon the Zealot**—trained as an assassin, but stunned to see his brother healed—rejects his zealot vows to join this new movement. He learns that Jesus doesn't need him but wants him. Jesus increasingly "stirs up the water," coming to the attention of the Roman authorities and Jewish religious leaders.

Episode 5: John the Baptist (the older cousin by six months) and Jesus have a sit-down conversation. **Mary Magdalene** struggles with PTSD from a close encounter with a Roman soldier and a demon-possessed man called **Legion** (real name, **Caleb**), who is delivered by Jesus. She ends up drawn back into her old lifestyle and leaves the group, who are very concerned about her disappearance. Jesus is as well, and sends Simon and Matthew to look for and, hopefully, return her.

Episode 6: Mary falls deeper into old habits, but Simon and Matthew find her and bring her back. She meets with Jesus, who is quick to extend forgiveness. The focus on love over law, and recovery over relapse, stands in sharp contrast to the views of the Pharisees, like **Shmuel**. They want to bring Jesus to 'justice' for what they see as blasphemy, as well as for healings and grain-eating (harvesting) on the Sabbath.

Episode 7: Andrew, despondent over John's imprisonment, leaves the group along with Philip. Jesus and his disciples prepare for an upcoming sermon to be witnessed by thousands. But that scenario appears to blow up when Roman soldiers lead Jesus away to Capernaum for questioning before **Quintus** (the Roman Praetor from Season One) and one of Caesar's cohorts, **Atticus**, who has been tailing Jesus.

Philip and Andrew come upon the Egyptian woman, **Tamar**, and the healed paralytic—both speaking about Jesus while Jesus is wanted for questioning. The episode ends with Jesus returning and the disciples asking him to teach them how to pray in the same manner that he does. Their desire to get "the heart and the mind right" pleases Jesus.

Episode 8: We anticipate the Big Reveal, as Jesus and Matthew work together on what will be called the *Sermon on the Mount* (Matthew 5-7). Jesus comes up with just the right introduction (the Beatitudes), while the disciples busy themselves with finding and negotiating the right spot, preparing leaflets, inviting townsfolk, welcoming old friends, and parents—plus crowd control. Thousands gather, including one who finds himself caught up in it all, **Judas (Iscariot)**. Jesus, decked out in a blue "Prince of Peace" sash, finally takes to the stage, and... the long-awaited Big Reveal will now be delivered in Season Three.

Looking Back on Season Three

Episode One: Jesus delivers the most life-altering, world-changing sermon in history. As a result, he gets more followers, more notoriety, and more enemies. **Matthew**, who earlier helped him to craft the *Sermon on the Mount* (Season Two, Episode 8), is now convicted by what he heard in the sermon. He realizes he must face his past and somehow reconcile with his parents. **Joanna**, married to Chuza, Herod Antipas' household manager, also hears the sermon, and gives **Andrew** the opportunity to visit **John the Baptist** in prison.

Episode Two: As Jesus draws crowds, the Roman leadership (**Quintus**), sees him as a problem. Pilgrims from all over descend on Capernaum and set up a tent city. As tensions rise on the home front (between **Simon** and **Eden**), Jesus empowers the twelve (now called "apostles") to go two-by-two and do his work of healing and preaching. This prompts **Little James** to ask why he hasn't been healed, bringing up the issue of suffering and seemingly unanswered prayer. Thomas is directed to go to the region where **Kafni** lives to ask for the hand of **Ramah** in marriage and "put in a good word for Jesus as well!"

Episode Three: Jesus' hometown of Nazareth is the scene of a festival where he sees old friends **Lazarus**, **Mary,** and **Martha.** He's asked to read the Scriptures by **Rabbi Benjamin** as a guest preacher in the local synagogue. Things turn deadly serious as his interpretation of Isaiah is seen as blasphemous; the hometown boy is driven by an angry synagogue mob to the edge of a cliff outside the city, to be killed. Jesus says, "this isn't going to happen" and walks through them unharmed.

Episode Four: The cast of main characters returns to Capernaum. We get a "taste and see" (black and white clips, no sound) of the two-by-two mission on which the disciples were sent. We also get a glimpse into the marital dynamics of **Simon and Eden.** Their conflict will feel very familiar to many couples. **Jairus,** his wife **Michal,** and his 12-year-old daughter **Nili** (who becomes ill from unclean city water), are introduced. We likewise get to know a woman with a continuous issue of blood (named **Veronica** here), setting the stage for two future healings.

Episode 5: Synagogue ruler, Jairus, intends to get his 12-year-old daughter healed, which means getting Jesus there in time. But Jesus' entourage is interrupted by **Veronica**, who'd suffered for 12 years with constant bleeding and caused her to be labeled as "unclean," excluded from society, but never from Jesus. Jesus must deal with competing demands, delays, and expectations.

Episode 6: Pilate hears about Jesus—from both his wife (Claudia, who dreamt of Jesus) and his colleague, **Atticus**. The disciples argue over tactics and tensions, prepare for worst-case scenarios, and try to quell the crisis their preaching in Decapolis has created. **Gaius'** loyalty is questioned by his Roman superior, **Quintus**, as Gaius shows sympathy to Jesus' followers. **Tamar** and **Mary Magdalene** disagree on how to show loyalty to Jesus with all that they are and have. **Andrew** and **Philip** handle a crisis involving Jesus' cousin, **John the Baptist,** languishing in prison but expressing doubts. **Simon the Zealot's** pursuers finally corner him and question his loyalty to Jesus and to their cause.

Episode 7: Big storylines ("Get used to different"), parables, and Jewish culture (feast of Purim, prayer tassels) set up the Finale! **Simon Peter** expresses his grief and anger at Jesus for allowing **Eden** to suffer; **John** must fetch him. **Zebedee**, his wife **Salome, Mary Magdalene**, and **Yussif,** help **Eden** process her own grief and marital issues. **Andrew and Philip** are in over their heads with a crisis that provokes Gentiles to riot, typified by **Nashan** and **Fatiyah. Thomas** returns without **Ramah**, who stays behind to "work on" her dad. **Matthew** denies, hides, and finally wears the Jewish roots of his faith. **Simon** sees that **Gaius'** slave, who is also his son, is sick, raising interest in "the Jewish doctor." Timely healings lead to a Feeding of the 5000 (Episode 8).

Episode 8: This season's Grand Finale focuses on feelings, food, and faith that God provides and cares for us in hard times. More healings, parables, and disputes among factions set up an epic miracle that involves Jesus and Jews breaking bread with quarrelsome Gentiles. Jesus is all-inclusive. **Jesus** walks on water and embraces the risk-taking, grief-stricken **Peter**. Rabbi **Shmuel** is invited to pray with Jesus. (Stay tuned for Season 4!) "Come to me all you who labor and are heavy laden" is Jesus' call after giving us all we can carry.

1. *Who is your favorite character(s) in Seasons One to Three? How has he or she been affected by their encounters with Jesus so far?*

—

—

**In this upcoming Chosen episode
Jesus comes up with a unique way for the disciples to
"sit shiva" for John the Baptist.**

BACKGROUND: *Sitting shiva* is a Jewish mourning practice which dates back to ancient times. The term "shiva" comes from the Hebrew word for seven, reflecting the practice's seven-day duration. After Jacob died, his son, Joseph, and the others (family plus Egyptian officials) observed a seven day mourning period (Genesis 50:7-11). Likewise, Job mourned his misfortune for seven days while sitting on the ground surrounded by "friends" (Job 2:11-13).

The mourning period usually begins immediately after the burial of the deceased and is observed by the immediate family members. Likewise, the community joins in to support the bereaved, offer condolences, and remember the deceased. Such a ritual serves to reinforce social bonds, offers a structured framework for mourning, and provides deeper spiritual and emotional support. It is characterized by:

Withdrawal from routine activities by the grieving mourners

Physical and outward signs of mourning

Community support of family, friends, and neighbors

Prayer and reflection on the value of life, morality, and memories

The end of shiva is marked by a gradual return to normal life, often symbolized by a walk outside the house by the mourners. This act served as a transition back into the broader community and the flow of daily life, although the full mourning period extends beyond shiva with additional practices and restrictions lasting for up to a year for parents.

INTRO: The word "shiva" means seven and stands for the traditional seven days of mourning by a Jewish family for the deceased. This episode of *The Chosen* begins with Jesus and his disciples "sitting shiva" for John the Baptist in a non-traditional way: they do it in what passes for John's "home"—the open road.

FROM *The* **CHOSEN**

1. *What do you think about the way John's memorial was celebrated?*

… What lessons did Jesus' disciples learn celebrating John's life?

DISCOVER Read > Mark > Discuss

INTRO: In Matthew 10, Jesus is preparing his disciples to go on a mission to Jewish towns with his message, "The kingdom of heaven is at hand." He warns them that they will face conflict and persecution.

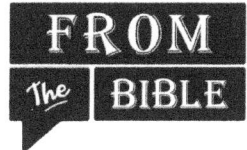

FROM *The* **BIBLE**

In the following passage, look for contrasts and conflicts.

Not Peace, but a Sword

MATTHEW 10 [34] "Do not think that I have come to bring peace to the earth. I have not come to bring peace, but a sword. [35] For I have come to set a man against his father, and a daughter against her mother, and a daughter-in-law against her mother-in-law. [36] And a person's enemies will be those of his own household. [37] Whoever loves father or mother more than me is not worthy of me, and whoever loves son or daughter more than me is not worthy of me. [38] And whoever does not take his cross and follow me is not worthy of me. [39] Whoever finds his life will lose it, and whoever loses his life for my sake will find it.

3. *What did you find disturbing about this passage?*

4. *How does the message of Jesus bring division in The Chosen?*

... in your world?

5. *What does Jesus require to follow him?*

WATCH View Episode 2B *(19 ½ min., 21:17 to 40:44)* > **Discuss**

INTRO: Caesarea Phillippi was a place known for its wickedness. The area was filled with temples and shrines dedicated to the Greek god, Pan. No devout Jew would dare to go near such an evil place, but Jesus brought his disciples there on a field trip.

FROM *The* **CHOSEN**

6. *Why did Jesus want his disciples to see "The Gates of Hell"?*

7. *Why do you think Jesus chose this place and time to ask the disciples about his identity?*

DISCOVER Read > Mark > Discuss **RELATE**

INTRO: REVIEW: We have come to the proverbial "fork in the road" with Jesus and his mission, as you see. Simon Peter's upcoming confession, *"You are the Christ, the Son of the living God,"* was a significant moment because Simon was no longer echoing the opinions of others but expressing his own beliefs.

FROM *The* **BIBLE**

What opinions about Jesus can you identify in the following passage?

Peter Confesses Jesus as the Christ
MATTHEW 16 [13] Now when Jesus came into the district of Caesarea Philippi, he asked his disciples, "Who do people say that the Son of Man is?"

[14] And they said, "Some say John the Baptist, others say Elijah, and others Jeremiah or one of the prophets."

[15] He said to them, "But who do you say that I am?"

[16] Simon Peter replied, "You are the Christ, the Son of the living God."

[17] And Jesus answered him, "Blessed are you, Simon Bar-Jonah! For flesh and blood has not revealed this to you, but my Father who is in heaven. [18] And I tell you, you are Peter, and on this rock I will build my church, and the gates of hell shall not prevail against it. [19] I will give you the keys of the kingdom of heaven, and whatever you bind on earth shall be bound in heaven, and whatever you loose on earth shall be loosed in heaven." [20] Then he strictly charged the disciples to tell no one that he was the Christ.

8. *How did Simon Peter's belief about Jesus differ from the beliefs of others?*

... What did he mean when he called Jesus, "the Christ"?

9. *Do you think the rock, or foundation, on which Jesus builds his church is Peter, his confession, or both?*

10. Keys open doors and only given to the most faithful servants. *How does Jesus giving them the keys to the kingdom confirm his trust?*

11. Being given "the keys" is also a way of delegating authority. *What are the "keys of the kingdom" in this context?*

    ... What do these keys do?

    ... How are they to be used by the disciples?

NOTE FOR EVERYONE: End by completing the RELATE questions and T-SHIRT DESIGN individually, and then share them with your group.

T-Shirt Design After watching > discovering > relating, What slogan would you write or draw on your T-Shirt?

Draft concepts or quotations for summarizing this section

Final design:

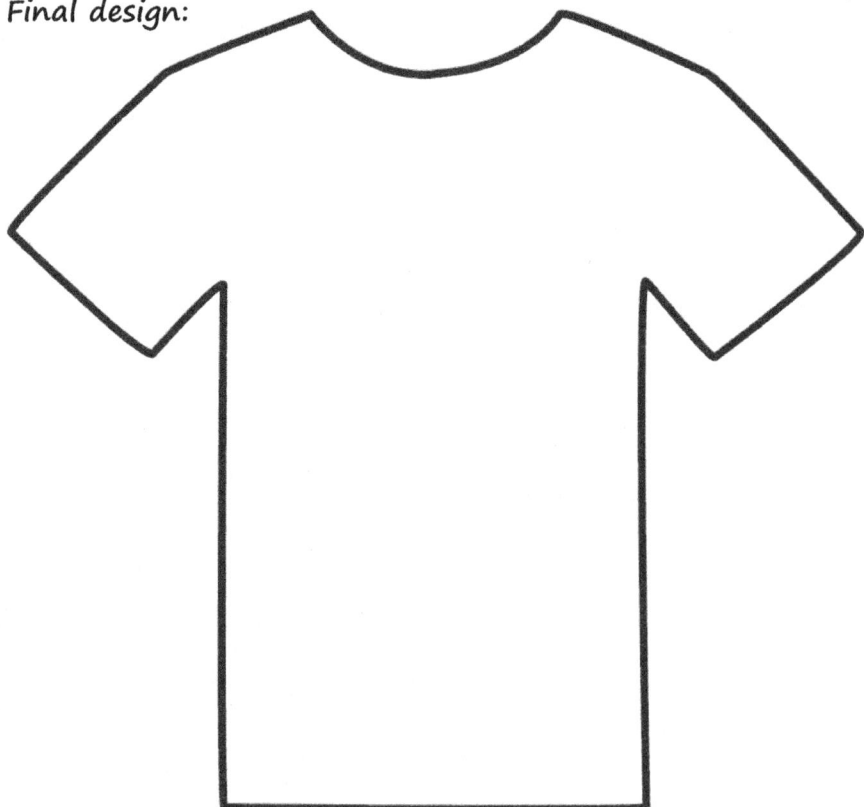

NOTES on Study #2 *Commentary and Historical Context*

Matthew 10:34-39 – Not Peace But a Sword

- The Prince of Peace wielding a sword sounds like a contradiction, but the peace Jesus brings is between God and the believer and between fellow believers. However, Christ also brings division between light and darkness, even between members of the same family.

- The Cross, like the sword, is an instrument of death, and in this case, symbolizes the call to make a total commitment as Christ followers.

Matthew 16:13-20 – Peter Confesses Jesus as the Christ

- Caesarea Philippi, built and renamed by Herod's son Philip, was located north of Galilee at the base of Mount Hermon. The city was originally named *Paneas* (after the Greek god Pan). This region was a center of pagan worship, thus an appropriate backdrop to confess Christ as the Rock that will prevail against the gates of Hades (the powers of death).

- Peter... rock... church is a play on words. In Greek, "Peter" is *petros* (little stone), while Jesus' community, the church is the "rock," *petra* (meaning bedrock).

Commentators have interpreted these words in four different ways. The bedrock is either: (1) the person of Christ; (2) Peter's confession, one that all true believers make; (3) Christ's teachings, a major emphasis in Matthew's Gospel; or (4) Peter himself, in accord with his role at Pentecost (Acts 2), with Cornelius (Acts 10), and his leadership among the apostles, which Paul regards as the bedrock (Ephesians 2:20). It is possible to see all four of these elements in Jesus' declaration.

- "Keys of the kingdom" enable one to announce guilt or innocence (see Matthew 18:18 in context); such keys also open the heart and mind to receive the grace of the gospel, especially for non-Jews.

REALISTIC *But* REAL?

That's plausible but did it happen?

If Jesus is divine, how come he shows such emotion, even conflicting emotions in grief? Jesus is also fully human, so he processes grief as we do—through dreams, talk with others, tears, and laughter—but also with the Jewish custom of *shiva* (mourning).

Is the way Jesus practiced Shiva for John that unusual? *Shiva* is the first period of structured mourning after death and is meant to help the mourners confront the reality of death. *The Chosen* depicts Jesus doing this by taking to the open road and bringing his followers to the "Gates of Hell." There, they can imagine John the Baptist standing up to the powers of sin. This too, will characterize their eventual ministry.

In using this occasion to also talk of marriage (between Thomas and Ramah) or other lighthearted issues, they were violating the etiquette of shiva but violating etiquette was not usual for Jesus!

Were any of the disciples married, or getting married, as the film depicts? Thomas and Ramah (a fictional character) have been paired up since Season One; and now they begin to talk of marriage, even involving Jesus in their planned matrimony. However, Simon is the only disciple recorded to be married (he had a mother-in-law, Mark 1:30). Paul does imply "other apostles" had wives (1 Corinthians 9:5), also an inference from Jewish culture, which assumed that most disciples of a rabbi were married.

Was there a literal "Gates of Hell"? Allegedly, yes, the place is near Caesarea Phillipi (Mount Hermon). The film accurately depicts pagan shrines to Baal and the cultic activity, even bestiality (implied with the goats in this film). This all happens outside the cave that the pagans considered an entrance into the underworld. At the altar of Pan outside the Gates of Hell, the disciples are rightly disgusted by "abominable" paganism and Jesus uses this occasion to communicate that, just as John was fearless to enter such disgusting conditions, so must they. In doing so, they will carry with them Jesus' power over sin and death.

Drive it Home Review and Respond: Worship, Pray, Share

Our world exhibits a great misconception of Jesus, especially those that focus on his "meek and mild" side. As Almighty God, co-creator of heaven and earth, as the one who stood up to the excruciating punishment of the Cross, and who will separate the sheep from goats at the final Judgment, Jesus is the lamb with the heart of a lion.

As Matthew 10 depicts, the *Prince of Peace* brought with him a sword... to start a war. The kingdom of heaven came invading the kingdom of darkness, and it was not going to be pretty.

The Way –Pat Barrett

Type in URL: tinyurl.com/the-way-song (4:19 min.)

Waymaker –Michael W. Smith

Type in URL: tinyurl.com/waymaker-song (4:04 min.)

10. *How would you answer Jesus' question regarding those you know, "Who do people say that the Son of Man is?"*

11. *How would you have answered Jesus' question, "But who do you say that I am?"*

... *How has your answer changed over time?*

Video Insights Why Jesus Came: To Bring a Sword –Colin Smith
Type in URL: tinyurl.com/matthew-10-34-39 (33:45 min.)
Thoughts:

_____

Who do you Say I Am? –Alistair Begg
Type in URL: tinyurl.com/who-do-you-say 27:06 min.)
Thoughts:

_____

Peter's Blessed Confession, Part 1 –Daniel Mayfield
Type in URL: tinyurl.com/peters-blessed-confession (1:40-12:40 min.)
Thoughts:

_____

A. C. T. S. Prayer:
Adoration / Confession / Thanksgiving / Supplication / Steps

Examine where you are with the Lord and the priority of his kingdom.
Take it to him in prayer:

ADORATION: How can you praise God from whom all blessings flow?

CONFESSION: What do you need to confess and change?

THANKSGIVING: Which circumstances will you thankfully embrace?

SUPPLICATION: For whom and for what will you pray?

Next STEPS: What will you do with what you've learned? With whom?

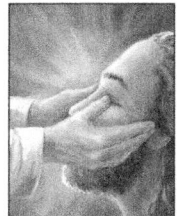

PRIOR To STUDY

A way to start the study and reminders

NOTE FOR LEADERS: Right before your group studies Matthew 5 (page 52), review the study process on pages 9-12—especially page 10 with the "W questions" and marking up the text with colored pens.

One way to **start your study** is to ask group members to share something they got out of the previous week's *Drive it Home* and *Video Insights* segments after the study.

When you begin the study of a passage, mention **the question or page on which to end**, so the group is reminded how far to go.

Evaluate as you proceed: What things are working well and what can be improved in your study and group discussion process?

Confessions, Part 2 (Ep. 2C)

Study #3

FROM *The* **BIBLE**

INTRO: Although Jesus' Sermon on the Mount was preached in the first episode of Season Three, its implications continue to affect the disciples' relationships in Season Four. In fact, the impact of that sermon continues to our day. In this study, we will return to Jesus' life-changing statements from Matthew 5.

DISCOVER Read Aloud > Mark It Up > Discuss

Look for what people have heard versus what Jesus says.

Anger
MATTHEW 5 [21] "You have heard that it was said to those of old, 'You shall not murder; and whoever murders will be liable to judgment.' [22] But I say to you that everyone who is angry with his brother will be liable to judgment; whoever insults his brother will be liable to the council; and whoever says, 'You fool!' will be liable to the hell of fire. [23] So if you are offering your gift at the altar and there remember that your brother has something against you, [24] leave your gift there before the altar and go. First be reconciled to your brother, and then come and offer your gift. . . .

Retaliation
MATTHEW 5 [38] "You have heard that it was said, 'An eye for an eye and a tooth for a tooth.' [39] But I say to you, Do not resist the one who is evil. But if anyone slaps you on the right cheek, turn to him the other also. [40] And if anyone would sue you and take your tunic, let him have your cloak as well. [41] And if anyone forces you to go one mile, go with him two miles. [42] Give to the one who begs from you, and do not refuse the one who would borrow from you.

Love Your Enemies
[43] "You have heard that it was said, 'You shall love your neighbor and hate your enemy.' [44] But I say to you, Love your enemies and pray for those who persecute you, [45] so that you may be sons of your Father who is in heaven. For he makes his sun rise on the evil and on the good, and sends rain on the just and on the unjust. [48] You therefore must be perfect, as your heavenly Father is perfect. . . .

1. *According to Jesus, why is anger dangerous?*

... How does he advise us to handle it?

2. *How does Jesus tell us to treat our enemies?*

3. *Jesus says, "You, therefore, must be perfect, as your heavenly Father is perfect" (Matthew 5:48)." What does he mean by this and how is it possible?*

| **WATCH** | **View Episode 2C** (26½min., 40:44 to 107:09) **> Discuss** |

INTRO: Anger, blame, and jealousy dominate the scenes. **Focus on how these conflicts are resolved.**

4. *How is conflict dealt with in this episode?*
   ... by Matthew, in his anger with Peter?

   ... by Big James and John, in their jealousy of Peter?

   ... by The Sanhedrin, in their anger and jealousy?

   ... by Quintus, in his anger and jealousy?

5. *How do the instructions Jesus gives to Matthew and Peter differ, and how are they the same?*

DISCOVER Read > Mark > Discuss RELATE

INTRO: Jesus was detailed and explicit in his directions about forgiveness to Matthew and Peter in this Chosen episode. Similarly, he tells us what to do in this passage from Matthew 18.

FROM
The **BIBLE**

Look for the similarities and differences between the characters.

If Your Brother Sins Against You
MATTHEW 18 [15] "If your brother sins against you, go and tell him his fault, between you and him alone. If he listens to you, you have gained your brother. [16] But if he does not listen, take one or two others along with you, that every charge may be established by the evidence of two or three witnesses. [17] If he refuses to listen to them, tell it to the church. And if he refuses to listen even to the church, let him be to you as a Gentile and a tax collector. . . . [20] For where two or three are gathered in my name, there am I among them."

The Parable of the Unforgiving Servant
[21] Then Peter came up and said to him, "Lord, how often will my brother sin against me, and I forgive him? As many as seven times?" [22] Jesus said to him, "I do not say to you seven times, but seventy-seven times. [23] "Therefore the kingdom of heaven may be compared to a king who wished to settle accounts with his servants. [24] When he began to settle, one was brought to him who owed him ten thousand talents. [25] And since he could not pay, his master ordered him to be sold, with his wife and children and all that he had, and payment to be made.

[26] So the servant fell on his knees, imploring him, 'Have patience with me, and I will pay you everything.' [27] And out of pity for him, the master

of that servant released him and forgave him the debt. ²⁸ But when that same servant went out, he found one of his fellow servants who owned him a hundred denarii, and seizing him, he began to choke him, saying, 'Pay what you owe.'

²⁹ So his fellow servant fell down and pleaded with him, 'Have patience with me, and I will pay you.' ³⁰ He refused and went and put him in prison until he should pay the debt. ³¹ When his fellow servants saw what had taken place, they were greatly distressed, and they went and reported to their master all that had taken place.

³² Then his master summoned him and said to him, 'You wicked servant! I forgave you all that debt because you pleaded with me. ³³ And should not you have had mercy on your fellow servant, as I had mercy on you?' ³⁴ And in anger his master delivered him to the jailers, until he should pay all his debt. ³⁵ So also my heavenly Father will do to every one of you, if you do not forgive your brother from your heart."

6. *What steps toward reconciliation does Jesus give us in Matthew 18?*

... What are the implications of his promise in verse 20?

7. *In Jesus' parable (Matthew 18:23-35), what did the king and his servant have in common and how are they different?*

8. Describe the source of the anger the king had for his servant.

... How is the king's anger like the anger of God?

T-Shirt Design After watching > discovering > relating, What slogan would you write or draw on your T-Shirt?

Draft concepts or quotations for summarizing this section:

Final design:

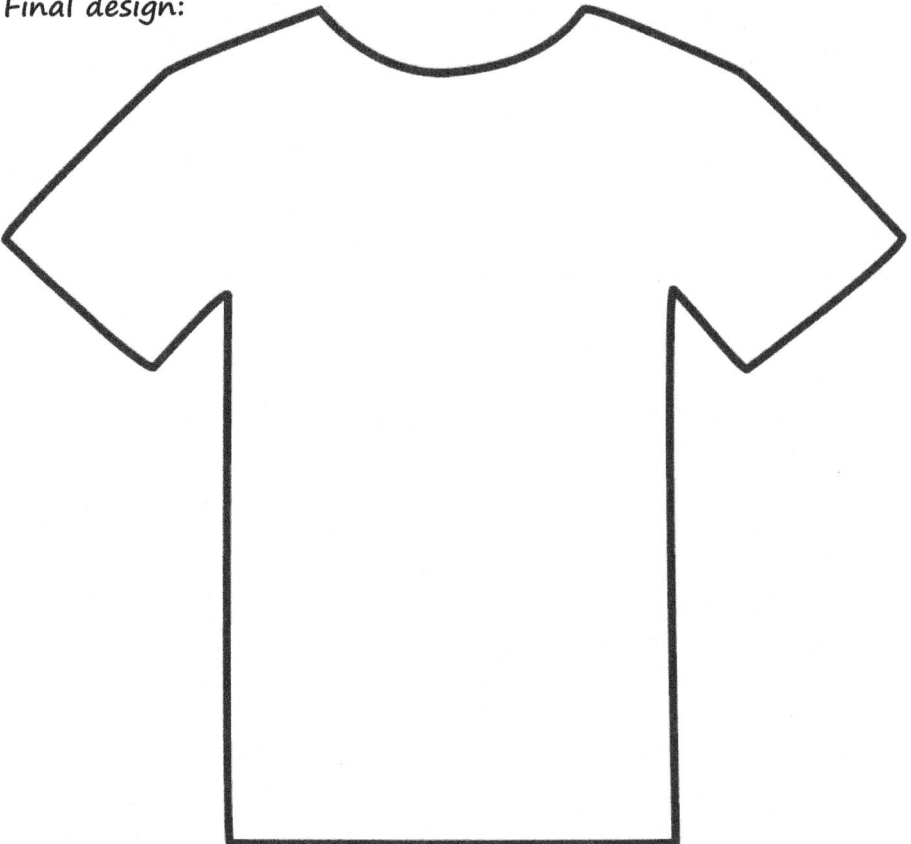

NOTES on Study #3 *Commentary and Historical Context*

Matthew 5:21-24; 38-42; 43-46 – Anger, Retaliation, and Love

- "You have heard… but I tell you." The contrast set up here (5:21,27,31,33,38,43) is not between Old Testament teaching, which Jesus had already affirmed as valid (5:17-18), but between the Pharisaic interpretation of the Old Testament and their practice of focusing on the eternals of the Law. True Old Testament teaching focused on the heart, which is exactly what Jeus meant to reaffirm.

- "Fire of hell" has both a literal meaning—referring to the perpetually burning city dump known in Greek as *Gehenna*, where human sacrifices to a pagan god were once offered—and later a figurative meaning, referring to the place of death and final punishment.

- The impetus to reconcile lies with the wrongdoer. It's pointless to go about business with God if your brother has something against you given that the business of God itself centers on reconciliation.

Matthew 18:15-35 – If Your Brother Sins Against You and Parable

- Here the impetus to reconcile lies with the offended party. The local congregation is to act like an appellate court if the offending brother will not listen to a legitimate grievance. Failure to reconcile ultimately then becomes a basis for excommunication.

- The Rabbis taught that one was obligated to forgive up to three times. Peter generously proposes "seven times." But Jesus counters with "seventy-seven times"; the expression could also mean "seventy times seven." In either event, Jesus lifts all limits on forgiveness!

- The parable Jesus tells also underscores this principle of forgiveness. The currency values in this parable point to the impossibility of ever repaying this debt to the fantastically wealthy king (a stand-in for God). A day's wage was just one denarius, so a Palestinian laborer would have had to work 15 years to earn enough denarii to equal one talent. However, this guy was responsible for 10,000 talents!

The servant forgiven such an impossibly huge debt should have shown mercy to a fellow servant with a significantly lesser obligation, just 100 denarii. By ironically failing to show even the slightest mercy, the first servant deservedly suffers the consequences.

REALISTIC But REAL?

That's plausible but did it happen?

Is the film accurate in depicting the attitude of the Sanhedrin toward Jesus? This Jewish Council of Elders—at this point in its cinematic arc— progresses from apathy to actively plotting Jesus' death for blasphemy (forgiving sins, a divine prerogative) and healing on the Sabbath. This Supreme Council (**The Sanhedrin**) during the New Testament era was consist of the chief priest, Caiaphas, plus 70 elders, elites and scribes.

Yussif, Jairus, Shammai, and Shmuel are plausible in their respective roles. With both a religious and political standing, the Sanhedrin stood against Jesus with the notable exception of Nicodemus (seen earlier in *The Chosen*) and Joseph of Arimathea (to be seen at the end). These two followers of Christ would have been the lone dissenters in the anti-Jesus movement represented by the Sanhedrin (Mark 15:43; Luke 23:50-51; John 3:1; 19:38-39).

Where in the Bible is the alleged conflict and forgiveness between Matthew and Peter? Scripture is silent on this, but not *The Chosen*. The film fleshes out Peter as the unforgiving protagonist, thus flipping the script of the parable of the Unmerciful Servant (Matthew 18:21-35). Simon Peter's grudge against Matthew dates to the terrible night in Season One, Episode 4, when he faced a debtor's prison for unpaid taxes monitored by Matthew. Thus, in this instance, Matthew (in the film) is the one who will not forgive the debt. But in Scripture (18:21), it is Simon Peter who questions why he should forgive "my brother."

Peter laments having to forgive even "seven times" for the multiple transgressions of Matthew (a Roman collaborator). Jesus insists that Peter forgive not just seven but "seventy times seven" (meaning, "endless forgiveness"). Interestingly, it is Matthew (who is both the unforgiving one and the forgiven one in the film) who records in Scripture Jesus' parable on forgiveness. Peter (the forgiver) hugs Matthew (the forgiven) as this episode ends. The film thus shows, more than tells, what biblical forgiveness looks like.

Drive it Home Review and Respond: Worship, Pray, Share

Resentment is the poison you drink thinking someone else is going to die. And forgiveness, well, listen carefully to the words in this first song and the story behind it.

Forgiveness –Matthew West
Type in URL: tinyurl.com/forgiveness-song (4:25 min.)

You Say –Lauren Daigle
Type in URL: tinyurl.com/you-say-song (4:30 min.)

9. *With whom do you need to forgive or be reconciled or who do you need to forgive?*

10. *Following Jesus' instructions, what is your next step in being reconciled to this person(s)?*

11. "Love your enemies and pray for those who persecute you" is not just a hard saying but impossible without the help of God's Spirit. *In what ways might this apply in your current circumstances?*

12. *What practical steps can you take to apply this commandment and to look to Jesus for his help in fulfilling it?*

Video Insights *What does the Bible say about anger?*
Type in URL: tinyurl.com/about-anger (4:48 min) *–Got Questions*
Thoughts: _____

The Keys To Conquer Anger and Bitterness *–John K. Jenkins*
Type in URL: tinyurl.com/conquer-anger (35:06 min.)
Thoughts: _____

What Does It Mean To Love Your Enemies? *–Jeffery Poor*
Type in URL: tinyurl.com/love-your-enemies (7:06)
Thoughts: _____

A. C. T. S. Prayer:
Adoration / Confession / Thanksgiving / Supplication / Steps

Examine where you are with the Lord and the priority of his kingdom. Take it to him in prayer:

ADORATION: How can you praise God from whom all blessings flow?

CONFESSION: What do you need to confess and change?

THANKSGIVING: Which circumstances will you thankfully embrace?

SUPPLICATION: For whom and for what will you pray?

Next STEPS: What will you do with what you've learned? With whom?

PRIOR To STUDY A universal need: spiritual sight

NOTE FOR EVERYONE:

Inviting new people—is it too late?

No, it isn't. One of the beautiful things about *The Chosen Study* is that new members can come in at any time and binge watch to catch up! Additionally, we've seen people go through each season's episodes multiple times.

Who to invite?

Anyone who fits on this list: friends, loved ones, family members, colleagues, teammates, acquaintances, those who cross your path—if they're curious, if they're willing to check it out—then invite them to come.

Moon to Blood (Episode 3)

Study #4

FROM *The* **BIBLE**

INTRO: The study guide cover, inspired by this episode, illustrates how important sight is to our lives. Our eyes, when properly functioning, help us see the world as it is. Likewise, when given the gift of spiritual sight, we can begin to see through the world's outer covering and into the kingdom purposes God has for our lives.

In this study, Jesus seeks to get this point across to his disciples and to the crowd. *"I am the light of the world,"* he declares... and he means for us to take him very seriously. Unless we are content to stumble around in darkness, we have no other option that will bring clarity to the reality that exists here and now, and beyond.

DISCOVER Read Aloud > Mark It Up > Discuss

Look for each of the statements made about Jesus.

Jesus Heals a Man Born Blind

JOHN 9 As he passed by, he saw a man blind from birth. [2] And his disciples asked him, "Rabbi, who sinned, this man or his parents, that he was born blind?"

[3] Jesus answered, "It was not that this man sinned, or his parents, but that the works of God might be displayed in him. [4] We must work the works of him who sent me while it is day; night is coming, when no one can work. [5] As long as I am in the world, I am the light of the world." [6] Having said these things, he spit on the ground and made mud with the saliva. Then he anointed the man's eyes with the mud [7] and said to him, "Go, wash in the pool of Siloam" (which means Sent). So he went and washed and came back seeing. . . .

[13] They brought to the Pharisees the man who had formerly been blind. [14] Now it was a Sabbath day when Jesus made the mud and opened his eyes. [15] So the Pharisees again asked him how he had received his sight. And he said to them, "He put mud on my eyes, and I washed, and I see."

[16] Some of the Pharisees said, "This man is not from God, for he does not keep the Sabbath." But others said, "How can a man who is a sinner do such signs?" And there was a division among them. [17] So they said again to the blind man, "What do you say about him, since he has opened your eyes?" He said, "He is a prophet."

[18] The Jews did not believe that he had been blind and had received his sight, until they called the parents of the man who had received his

sight [19] and asked them, "Is this your son, who you say was born blind? How then does he now see?"

[20] His parents answered, "We know that this is our son and that he was born blind. [21] But how he now sees we do not know, nor do we know who opened his eyes. Ask him; he is of age. He will speak for himself." [22] (His parents said these things because they feared the Jews, for the Jews had already agreed that if anyone should confess Jesus to be Christ, he was to be put out of the synagogue.) [23] Therefore his parents said, "He is of age; ask him."

[24] So for the second time they called the man who had been blind and said to him, "Give glory to God. We know that this man is a sinner." [25] He answered, "Whether he is a sinner I do not know. One thing I do know, that though I was blind, now I see." [26] They said to him, "What did he do to you? How did he open your eyes?"

[27] He answered them, "I have told you already, and you would not listen. Why do you want to hear it again? Do you also want to become his disciples?"

[28] And they reviled him, saying, "You are his disciple, but we are disciples of Moses. [29] We know that God has spoken to Moses, but as for this man, we do not know where he comes from."

[30] The man answered, "Why, this is an amazing thing! You do not know where he comes from, and yet he opened my eyes. [31] We know that God does not listen to sinners, but if anyone is a worshiper of God and does his will, God listens to him. [32] Never since the world began has it been heard that anyone opened the eyes of a man born blind. If this man were

not from God, he could do nothing." [34] They answered him, "You were born in utter sin, and would you teach us?" And they cast him out.

1. *What do you learn from verses 1-7 about the reasons for suffering?*

2. *What preconceptions kept the Pharisees from recognizing that Jesus had come from God?*

3. *Why did the formerly blind man's parents refuse to stand up for their son?*

4. Read verses 17, 24-25, and 31-33. *How does the formerly blind man move from ignorance to faith?*

WATCH View Episode 3 (53 ½ min.., :44 to 54:00) > Discuss

INTRO: All our actions affect other people. Just as Jesus' healing of the blind man led to various outcomes in this episode, we will see how the decisions each character makes leads to unforeseen and unintended consequences for themselves and for others.

FROM
The CHOSEN

5. *How did the actions of each of the following characters change the circumstances of someone else?*

... David's sin with Bathsheba?

... Atticus' pitting of Gaius against Quintus?

... Jesus' decision to heal Uzziah?

... John preventing James from attacking Quintus?

6. *How do you see Jesus orchestrating events?*

DISCOVER Read > Mark > Discuss RELATE

INTRO: Jesus had harsh words for the Jewish leaders, whom he called blind guides, greedy, and hypocritical. When he said in the video, "I'm just getting started," that was certainly the case.

FROM
The BIBLE

Look for and identify Jesus' accusations against the Jewish leaders.

Seven Woes to the Scribes and Pharisees
MATTHEW 23 Then Jesus said... ² "The scribes and the Pharisees sit on Moses' seat, ³ so do and observe whatever they tell you, but not the works they do. For they preach, but do not practice.

⁴ They tie up heavy burdens, hard to bear, and lay them on people's shoulders, but they themselves are not willing to move them with their finger. ⁵ They do all their deeds to be seen by others. For they make their phylacteries broad and their fringes long, ⁶ and they love the place of honor at feasts and the best seats in the synagogues ⁷ and greetings in the marketplaces and being called rabbi by others.

[8] But you are not to be called rabbi, for you have one teacher, and you are all brothers. [9] And call no man your father on earth, for you have one Father, who is in heaven. [10] Neither be called instructors, for you have one instructor, the Christ. [11] The greatest among you shall be your servant. [12] Whoever exalts himself will be humbled, and whoever humbles himself will be exalted.

[13] "But woe to you, scribes and Pharisees, hypocrites! For you shut the kingdom of heaven in people's faces. For you neither enter yourselves nor allow those who would enter to go in. [15] Woe to you, scribes and Pharisees, hypocrites! For you travel across sea and land to make a single proselyte, and when he becomes a proselyte, you make him twice as much a child of hell as yourselves.

[16] "Woe to you, blind guides, who say, 'If anyone swears by the temple, it is nothing, but if anyone swears by the gold of the temple, he is bound by his oath.' [17] You blind fools! For which is greater, the gold or the temple that has made the gold sacred?. . .

[23] "Woe to you, scribes and Pharisees, hypocrites! For you tithe mint and dill and cumin, and have neglected the weightier matters of the law: justice and mercy and faithfulness. These you ought to have done, without neglecting the others. [24] You blind guides, straining out a gnat and swallowing a camel!

[25] "Woe to you, scribes and Pharisees, hypocrites! For you clean the outside of the cup and the plate, but inside they are full of greed and self-indulgence. [26] You blind Pharisee! First clean the inside of the cup and the plate, that the outside also may be clean.

²⁷ "Woe to you, scribes and Pharisees, hypocrites! For you are like whitewashed tombs, which outwardly appear beautiful, but within are full of dead people's bones and all uncleanness. ²⁸ So you also outwardly appear righteous to others, but within you are full of hypocrisy and lawlessness.

²⁹ "Woe to you, scribes and Pharisees, hypocrites! . . .

³³ You serpents, you brood of vipers, how are you to escape being sentenced to hell?. . .

7. *According to Jesus, how have the Jewish leaders failed to lead?*

8. *What does Jesus claim has consumed the interest of these leaders?*

9. *What has Jesus taught you about leading in God's kingdom?*

T-Shirt Design After watching > discovering > relating, What slogan would you write or draw on your T-Shirt?

Draft concept:

Final design:

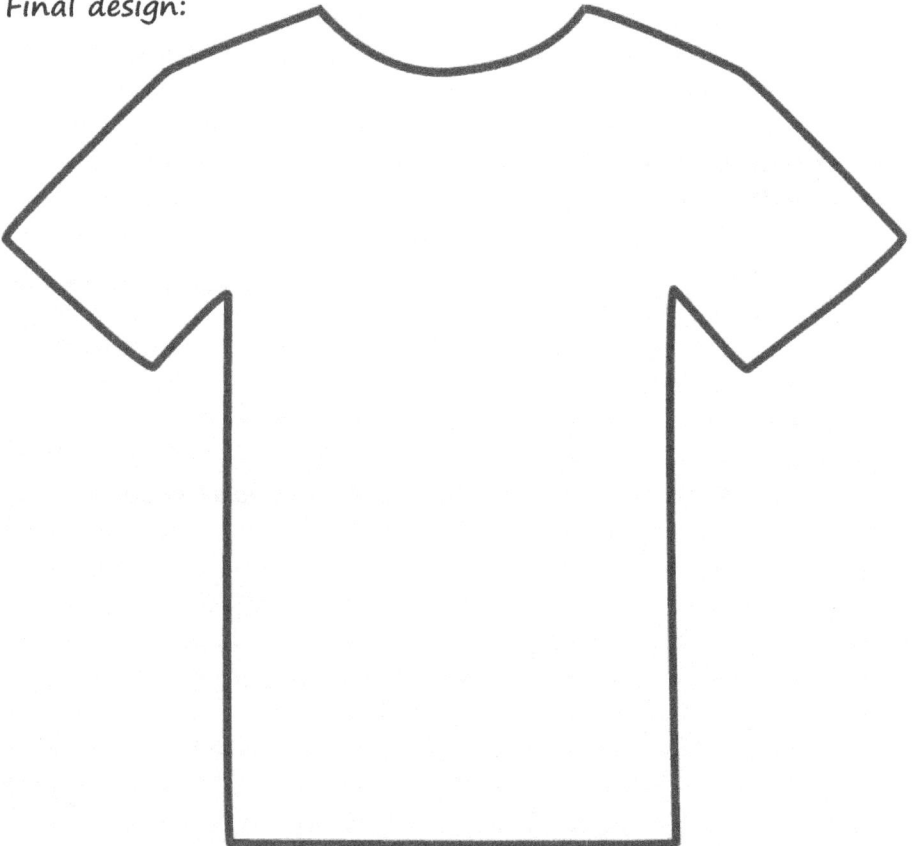

Commentary and Historical Context

John 9:1-34 – Jesus Heals a Man Born Blind

- The rabbis taught that suffering had its root cause in sin--either that of the victim or the victim's parents. One born blind could have sinned in utero or in a previous life—or so they believed. Jesus flatly denies this mindset.

- Healing the blind is predictive of the Messiah to come (Isaiah 29:18; 35:5; 42:7), thus demonstrating Jesus is the *"light of the world."* Yet these Jewish leaders were oblivious to this sign, showing themselves to be spiritually blind.

- For one unschooled in such matters, the newly sighted man rightly infers, contrary to his interrogators, that Jesus is from God. His parents, not wanting to suffer potential consequences from the authorities, defer to their son regarding what obviously took place. Their son's simple insistence on the facts, and what they meant about Jesus' identity, earned his interrogators' wrath.

Matthew 23:1-33 – Seven Woes to the Scribes and Pharisees

- A "phylactery" was a box, tied into one's hair, that contained four Scriptures (Exodus 13:1-10; 13:11-16; Deuteronomy 6:4-9; 11:13-21).

- Jesus condemns not the zeal of the Pharisees, but the outcome of their proselytizing. He claims they burden their converts with so much legalism, devoid of true spirituality, that they become bound for hell ("a son of hell").

- Jesus is not opposed to obeying the minutia of the Law, but rather the hypocrisy of thereby neglecting weightier matters of the Law.

- It was considered a sin to step on a tomb accidentally; hence tombs were whitewashed to make them more visible to passersby.

- The expression "from Abel to Zechariah" was like our expression, "from A to Z," or "from Genesis to Revelation." Jesus was thus holding Jewish leaders responsible for all the martyrdom perpetrated on the prophets in the Old Testament.

REALISTIC But REAL? | That's plausible but did it happen?

Were James and John self-promoting, or did their mom advocate for them to get offices in God's kingdom? Both, it seems. Whereas Simon Peter is given a new name and status (see previous episode), James and John are not similarly "promoted." They feel slighted yet don't want to stir things up. But their mother is unhappy and not a little bit pushy. She urges them to "ask" ("and they will receive") it. The gospels record that the boys took up their cause with Jesus (Mark 10:35-45) and that their mother also intervened for them (Matthew 20:20-28).

Is this how the healing of the man born blind happened?
The film follows the account from John 9 closely, with but a few minor variations. In the film, a random person asks Jesus the pivotal question of causation, while in the Gospels, the question about blindness is posed by the disciples. In the film, Big James brings water for cleansing after Jesus puts mud on the eyes of the man (named Uzziah, in the film). In the Gospels, that man is sent off to the Pool of Siloam to wash.

The mystery remains: God allows disability and death, and heals some, not others. In the film, as in the gospels, healing on the Sabbath stirs up controversy, especially with the Pharisees over Jesus and his mission.

What are we to make of the accidental killing of Ramah, who does not appear in Scripture? While her killing is unintended, her death fits the larger narrative arc of the film and Jesus' purpose in the Gospels. Her death is juxtaposed with the continuing disability of Little James, the healing of the man born blind, the raising of Lazarus, and the death of King David's firstborn (in the prologue to this episode). All to say that God heals some but not others, not even beloved Ramah.

Would Jesus have said, "It is not her time. I'm sorry"? The character of Ramah is fictional, not in Scripture. However, whether Jesus would have said this is unknown. Her "time" could refer to future healing at the resurrection (Matthew 22:31; Luke 14:14; 20:35; John 11:24). Or, it could also refer to the undying love between Thomas and Ramah (in the film, "until the end of time"). In either event, such references are of no comfort to Thomas, who wants Jesus to "fix this mistake" and bring her back to life now.

Drive it Home Review and Respond: Worship, Pray, Share

Review the study. The song is a remake of a well-known hymn written by John Newton. As a slave trader and captain, he nearly lost his life in a shipwreck but later received God's mercy for the terrible things he had done. He became a minister and penned these famous words as a "spiritual autobiography in verse" for a sermon at his 1773 New Years' service at the Church of St. Peter and St. Paul. The tune would not be written for another half-century but has endured as a profound descripttion of so many people's experiences of God's grace.

Amazing Grace (My Chains are Gone) –Chris Tomlin
Type in URL tinyurl.com/tomlin-grace (5:47min.)

This Is Our God –Phil Wickham
Type in URL tinyurl.com/this-is-our-God (4:32min.)

10. In the video, Salome quotes Jesus' promise, *"Ask and it will be given to you; seek and you will find; knock and it will be opened to you,"* (Matthew 7:7) to prompt James and John to ask to rule in Jesus' kingdom. *How did she misinterpret Jesus' words?*

11. *What may we ask Jesus to give us?*

... For what have you been asking?

... Have you asked him? Why or why not?

Video Insights *Blind from Birth* –Alistair Begg
Type in URL: tinyurl.com/John-9-Begg (34:06 min.)
Thoughts:

_____

Matthew 23 Summary in 5 minutes –2BeLikeChrist
Type in URL: tinyurl.com/matthew-23 (4:34 min.)
Thoughts:

_____

God's Hidden Message: Miracle of the Blind Man –Rabbi Jason Sobel
Type in URL: tinyurl.com/born-blind (12:30 min.)
Thoughts:

_____

A. C. T. S. Prayer:

Adoration / Confession / Thanksgiving / Supplication / Steps

Examine where you are with the Lord and the priority of his kingdom. Take it to him in prayer:

ADORATION: How can you praise God from whom all blessings flow?

CONFESSION: What do you need to confess and change?

THANKSGIVING: Which circumstances will you thankfully embrace?

SUPPLICATION: For whom and for what will you pray?

Next STEPS: What will you do with what you've learned? With whom?

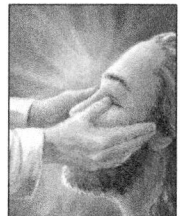

PRIOR **To STUDY**

Plan ahead now for your last (11th) study!

FOR LEADERS AND EVERYONE: There are some helpful and fun options for planning an 11th study. Please check out page 132 now to acquaint yourself with these options.

If you and your group decide to do something *different* than a normal (11th) meeting, make sure everyone checks their schedules. You want as many of your members there as possible. Again, check out page 132!

Calm Before (Episode 4)

Study #5

INTRO: There is no escaping grief. In this first section of Episode 4, we are invited to grieve with Thomas, Jesus, and the disciples as they travel to return Ramah's body to her father, Kafni.

FROM The **CHOSEN**

WATCH **View Episode 4A** *(16 min.., 0:21 to 16:13)* > **Discuss**

INTRO: As you watch Episode 4, think about the questions and problems faced by each character. *Where are they looking for answers?*

1. *What issues are troubling each of the following characters?*
   Peter?

   Mary Magdalene?

   John?

   Thomas?

   … How are they attempting to solve their issues?

WATCH **View Episode 4B** *(34 min.., 17:14 to 51:14)* > **Discuss**

INTRO: The most important decision in anyone's life is how they will respond to Jesus. The darkness of Ramah's death is interrupted, at least temporarily, by the joy of new spiritual birth.

DISCOVER **Read Aloud** > **Mark It Up** > **Discuss**

INTRO: Matthew 8:5-13 comes amid stories of miraculous healings. It is significant because this one was done from a distance and for a Gentile.

FROM *The* **BIBLE**

Look for words that name or describe characteristics that cannot be seen or touched.

The Faith of a Centurion
MATTHEW 8 [5] When he had entered Capernaum, a centurion came forward to him, appealing to him, [6] "Lord, my servant is lying paralyzed at home, suffering terribly."

[7] And he said to him, "I will come and heal him."

[8] But the centurion replied, "Lord, I am not worthy to have you come under my roof, but only say the word, and my servant will be healed. [9] For I too am a man under authority, with soldiers under me. And I say to one, 'Go,' and he goes, and to another, 'Come,' and he comes, and to my servant, 'Do this,' and he does it."

[10] When Jesus heard this, he marveled and said to those who followed him, "Truly, I tell you, with no one in Israel have I found such faith. [11] I tell you, many will come from east and west and recline at table with Abraham, Isaac, and Jacob in the kingdom of heaven, [12] while the sons of the kingdom will be thrown into the outer darkness. In that place there will be weeping and gnashing of teeth." [13] And to the centurion Jesus said, "Go; let it be done for you as you have believed." And the servant was healed at that very moment.

2. *What does the centurion understand about himself?*

... about Jesus?

3. *Why does Jesus "marvel" in verse 10?*

4. *How does Jesus use the centurion's request to teach about the kingdom of heaven?*

WATCH View Episode 4C *(11 min., 51:14 to 102:16)* > **Discuss**

INTRO: Changing people's long-held perceptions can be difficult and discouraging, yet this was a critical task Jesus came to accomplish. As you watch this next scene, think about how you would explain the kingdom of God to people who had long been expecting a political kingdom.

DISCOVER Read > Mark > Discuss **RELATE**

INTRO: It is said that there is no such thing as a bad question, but perhaps that is not always true. Sometimes it may be best to know for what we are "asking" before opening our mouths!

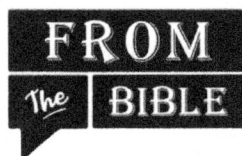

FROM *The* **BIBLE**

Look for contrasts between Jesus' words and the expectations of James and John.

Jesus Foretells His Death a Third Time

MARK 10 ³² And they were on the road, going up to Jerusalem, and Jesus was walking ahead of them. And they were amazed, and those who followed were afraid. And taking the twelve again, he began to tell them what was to happen to him, ³³ saying, "See, we are going up to Jerusalem, and the Son of Man will be delivered over to the chief priests and the scribes, and they will condemn him to death and deliver him over to the Gentiles. ³⁴ And they will mock him and spit on him, and flog him and kill him. And after three days he will rise."

The Request of James and John

³⁵ And James and John, the sons of Zebedee, came up to him and said to him, "Teacher, we want you to do for us whatever we ask of you."

³⁶ And he said to them, "What do you want me to do for you?" ³⁷ And they said to him, "Grant us to sit, one at your right hand and one at your left, in your glory."

[38] Jesus said to them, "You do not know what you are asking. Are you able to drink the cup that I drink, or to be baptized with the baptism with which I am baptized?"

[39] And they said to him, "We are able."

And Jesus said to them, "The cup that I drink you will drink, and with the baptism with which I am baptized, you will be baptized, [40] but to sit at my right hand or at my left is not mine to grant, but it is for those for whom it has been prepared." [41] And when the ten heard it, they began to be indignant at James and John.

[42] And Jesus called them to him and said to them, "You know that those who are considered rulers of the Gentiles lord it over them, and their great ones exercise authority over them. [43] But it shall not be so among you. But whoever would be great among you must be your servant, [44] and whoever would be first among you must be slave of all. [45] For even the Son of Man came not to be served but to serve, and to give his life as a ransom for many."

5. *How does Jesus' description of future events differ from the expectations of James and John?*

6. *Why did the other disciples become indignant?*

7. *What do Jesus' words teach us about greatness?*

T-Shirt Design After watching > discovering > relating, What slogan would you write or draw on your T-Shirt?

Draft concepts:

Final design:

NOTE FOR EVERYONE: If you haven't engaged with the *Drive it Home* section yet (pages 85-87), no problem. Consider it as an opportunity to establish "a Sabbath" by carving out time to review and respond to the previous study's content. (What day and time are best for you?) After looking back over the last study, engage with the worship videos provided. Go deeper with additional video insights. Share and encourage others in your group from your experience.

NOTES on Study #5 *Commentary and Historical Context*

Matthew 8:5-13 – The Faith of a Centurion
- A centurion was a Roman military officer in charge of 100 soldiers.

- The centurion's confession, "I do not deserve," echoes John the Baptist who, upon meeting Jesus, famously said, "I am not fit" (3:1). It is the epitome of those who are "poor in spirit" (Matthew 5:3).

- Jesus' healing the centurion typifies the universality of the gospel. Gentiles from "east and west," not just Jews from Israel, will enter God's kingdom and feast with Abraham and his descendants. Jesus is quick to point out the irony that this man has more faith than any he has seen in Israel. He becomes the model for the disciples of what it means to wholeheartedly trust Jesus.

Mark 10:32-34 – Jesus Foretells His Death a Third Time
- "Again" (for the third time; see 9:12,31) Jesus tells the Twelve, his closest followers, about his imminent betrayal, arrest, humiliation, torture, and execution. They obviously didn't want to hear what he was clearly saying. Only after the resurrection would they finally see the truth of why it was imperative (to satisfy God's justice and to provide for our reconciliation) that he suffered and die.

Mark 10:35-45 – The Request of James and John
- This audacious request shows how much the disciples were still missing about the nature of Jesus' mission.

- In Matthew's version (10:20-28), it is their mother who dares to request this leadership role for her two sons. It is interesting and quite relevant for today how *The Chosen* portrays misinterpreting what it means to "ask, seek, knock" (Matthew 7:7-12)!

 Whoever is behind the request—likely both mother and sons in different ways—Jesus uses this occasion to define servant leadership, a lifestyle of critical importance for the disciples to learn as his ambassadors.

REALISTIC But REAL?

That's plausible but did it happen?

The grief shared by Jesus and the disciples for Thomas and Kafni is palpable, but did it happen? A very plausible and complex story of grief is built around the fictional character of Ramah. Complex grief is best dealt with, then and now, with our presence more than our words. Inadequacy (felt by Peter and John), guilt (in Mary Magdalene and Thomas), and anger (in Ramah's father, Kafni) compound the grief. That all makes it more complex and harder to recover from.

This jumble of emotions is plausibly portrayed in the film and embraced by Jesus, but no such incident is recorded in the Bible. No doubt such incidents happened, as Jesus did not raise everyone from the dead, nor did God answer every prayer for healing with a *"Yes,"* but more often with a *"No"* or *"Wait."*

Is Jesus' humanness overdone by showing him frustrated, needing comfort, and yearning for simpler times? Probably not if, as we believe, he was *fully* human. For instance, as the lead disciples behave as juveniles debating food etiquette, Jesus (annoyed) leaves to be comforted by Little James and Thaddeus.

When James and John finally get around to asking for seats at Jesus' right and left hand (invoking pre-eminent authority, which occurred in Mark 10:35-45), Jesus is perturbed by how little they understand servant-leadership in the kingdom. He rightly wonders what else he must do to get through to them. What is more, Jesus doesn't just give hugs, but in weakness, he cries, *"My friends and companions stand aloof"* (Psalm 38:11). As if in answer to that prayer, God sends Gaius to hug Jesus (in *The Chosen*), who is thus comforted.

Did the healing of the centurion's servant/son happen as portrayed in the film, or were there creative liberties? Yes, and yes. The film version conflates the three biblical accounts very faithfully and creatively in adding that the servant/son was a child out of wedlock.

Drive it Home *Review and Respond: Worship, Pray, Share*

Review the study. Who among us doesn't want to be great? And there is nothing wrong with such a pursuit. It's just that within Jesus' upside-down kingdom *"whoever would be great among you must be your servant, and whoever would be first among you must be slave of all"* (Mark 10:43-44). So, greatness comes from taking up the rear and being the one who helps others succeed. Maybe, even likely, we end up going unnoticed in the process… but not by Everyone!

Confidence –Sanctus Real
Type in URL: tinyurl.com/the-confidence-song (3:15 min.)

Scars –I Am They
Type in URL: tinyurl.com/scars-song (3:57 min.)

8. *Is there someone whom you admire as a person with Jesus' values of servant-leadership? What particularly impresses you?*

In what ways have you pursued significance or greatness?

9. *… How does your pursuit compare to the things Jesus' taught in this study?*

Video Insights The #1 Reason... (Mark 10) –Brandon Robbins
Type in URL: tinyurl.com/James-John-ask (30:46 min.)
Thoughts:
_____

How are faith and authority related? –Martin Bender
Type in URL: tinyurl.com/authority-and-faith (6:48 min.)
Thoughts:
_____

What does putting God first really mean? –GotQuestions.org
Type in URL: tinyurl.com/putting-God-first (5:02 min.)
Thoughts:
_____

A. C. T. S. Prayer:

Adoration / Confession / Thanksgiving / Supplication / Steps

Examine where you are with the Lord and the priority of his kingdom. Take it to him in prayer:

ADORATION: How can you praise God from whom all blessings flow?

CONFESSION: What do you need to confess and change?

THANKSGIVING: Which circumstances will you thankfully embrace?

SUPPLICATION: For whom and for what will you pray?

Next STEPS: What will you do with what you've learned? With whom?

PRIOR To STUDY

Getting ready now for your last gathering.

NOTE FOR LEADERS: It may prove helpful to consider the study process again with your group (pages 10-11), especially the use of the "W questions." These questions make for a useful starting point for personal study, along with the LOOK FOR clues given after the INTRO.

Always read the INTRO and the PASSAGE aloud. Either do so yourself or find someone in the group who is a good reader. For the longer passages, you can assign more than one reader to break up the text.

Keep up the pace. You often think you have more time than you do, so, closely monitor your time, leave things unsaid, even skip questions, if necessary. The total watch time of this episode (an hour!) is rather long so... well you know... keep moving... to finish... on time!

Sitting, Serving, Scheming (Episode 5)

Study #6

INTRO: To serve or be served, to receive honor or to give it. These are key differences between the kingdom of God and the kingdoms of this world. The clash of these kingdoms will become more and more apparent in today's study.

FROM The CHOSEN

WATCH View Episode 5 (28 min., from .20 to 28:00) > Discuss

INTRO: Note the application of Matthew 5:41, 44: "And if anyone forces you to go one mile, go with him two miles. . . . I say to you, *Love your enemies and pray for those who persecute you.*"

1. *How did the various disciples react to being conscripted to carry the Roman soldier's equipment?*

2. *How does Jesus' reaction compare to theirs... and to ours?*

DISCOVER Read Aloud > Mark It Up > Discuss

INTRO: This episode includes debate among two Jewish leadership factions, the Pharisees with their more literal interpretation of Scripture and the Sadducees who came from the wealthy class.

FROM The BIBLE

BACKGROUND: Jesus entered such discussions when they served to help him correct the truth of God's Word. A case in point not addressed in this episode, but a good example, is the practice of *Corban* which was a vow to dedicate one's possessions only to God.

Sounds good, right?! The problem came when adult children (with their religious leaders' backing) used it as an excuse to disregard the 5th commandment (*"honor your father and mother,"* Exodus 20:12). So, even if their parents slipped into financial stress and poverty, they could continue to use their wealth and possessions only for themselves and thus avoid helping their parents by claiming that the vow dedicated these resources to be spent only for future religious purposes.

The Pharisees encouraged the abuse of this vow because they desired access to all such funds. Jesus didn't condemn the vow itself, but he did condemn such an application of it, calling it "the traditions of men" (Mark 7:8). It is an interesting exercise to consider what we do today that would be practicing "our traditions" versus God's values!

Look for the contrast between Jesus' values and those of the Pharisees.

Traditions and Commandments

MARK 7 Now when the Pharisees gathered to him, with some of the scribes who had come from Jerusalem, ² they saw that some of his disciples ate with hands that were defiled, that is, unwashed. ³ (For the Pharisees and all the Jews do not eat unless they wash their hands properly, holding to the tradition of the elders, ⁴ and when they come from the marketplace, they do not eat unless they wash. And there are many other traditions that they observe, such as the washing of cups and pots and copper vessels and dining couches.)

⁵ And the Pharisees and the scribes asked him, "Why do your disciples not walk according to the tradition of the elders, but eat with defiled hands?" ⁶ And he said to them, "Well did Isaiah prophesy of you hypocrites, as it is written,

"'This people honors me with their lips,

but their heart is far from me;

⁷ in vain do they worship me,

teaching as doctrines the commandments of men.'

⁸ You leave the commandment of God and hold to

the tradition of men."

⁹ And he said to them, "You have a fine way of rejecting the commandment of God in order to establish your tradition! ¹⁰ For Moses said, 'Honor your father and your mother'; and, 'Whoever reviles father or mother must surely die.' ¹¹ But you say, 'If a man tells his father or his mother, "Whatever you would have gained from me is Corban"' (that is, given to God) — ¹² then you no longer permit him to do anything for

his father or mother, [13] thus making void the word of God by your tradition that you have handed down. And many such things you do."

3. *What traditions did the Pharisees think Jesus should keep and why?*

4. *Why did Jesus call the Pharisees hypocrites?*

5. *What is the difference between religious tradition and God's commandments?*

… How might some of our "traditions" prevent us from obeying God?

WATCH **View Episode 5B** (17 min., 28:00 to 44:58) **> Discuss**

INTRO: Lazarus and his sisters are portrayed as a close family, but even loving families have their conflicts. **Look for examples of joy and conflict as you watch the next section of the episode.**

FROM The **CHOSEN**

6. *What did you find appealing about the household of Lazarus?*

… What personality conflicts did you notice?

DISCOVER Read > Mark > Discuss RELATE

INTRO: Just in case you missed the conflict between Mary and Martha, we will take a look at the Bible's account of it in Luke 10:38-42.

FROM The BIBLE

Look for contrasts between the two sisters.

Martha and Mary

LUKE 10 [38] Now as they went on their way, Jesus entered a village. And a woman named Martha welcomed him into her house. [39] And she had a sister called Mary, who sat at the Lord's feet and listened to his teaching.

[40] But Martha was distracted with much serving. And she went up to him and said, "Lord, do you not care that my sister has left me to serve alone? Tell her then to help me."

[41] But the Lord answered her, "Martha, Martha, you are anxious and troubled about many things, [42] but one thing is necessary. Mary has chosen the good portion, which will not be taken away from her."

7. *What do you find to admire... about Martha?*

... about Mary?

8. *What does Jesus say is the most important priority? Why?*

WATCH View Episode 5C (19 min., 44:58 to 104:19) > **Discuss**

INTRO: The remainder of this episode is not in the gospels. So, if you do not have time, group members can watch it on their own. However, if you do have time, it includes two interesting conversations, one between Jesus and his Eema, and the other between Judas and Hadad. Below are some discussion questions.

Notice how each of them reflects different priorities and values.

8. *What concerns does Jesus express to his mother as she washes his hair?*

9. *Why has Judas become uncomfortable with Jesus?*

... What does he understand about Jesus?

... What does he not understand?

T-Shirt Design After watching > discovering > relating, What slogan would you write or draw on your T-Shirt?

Draft concepts:

Final design:

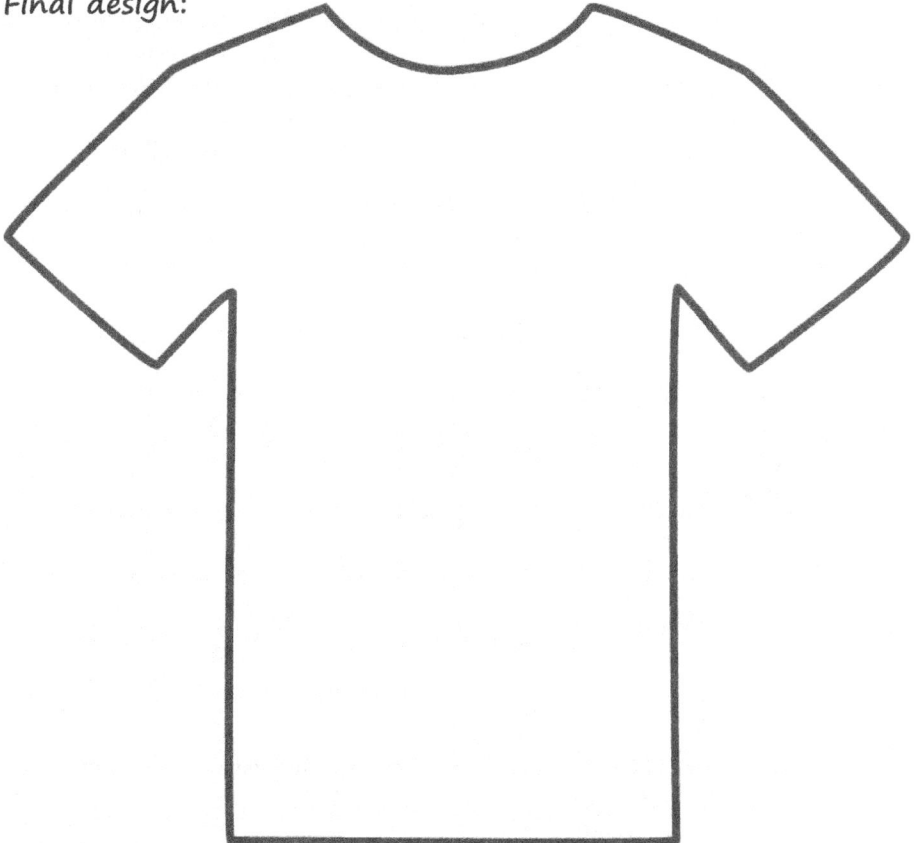

NOTES on Study #6 Commentary and Historical Context

Mark 7:1-13 – Traditions and Commandments

• Jesus vehemently disagreed with how religious leaders of his day sought to *protect* people from violating OT law by adding a hedge of guidelines around it called *The Tradition of the Elders*. Thirty-nine subcategories of regulations (!) pertained just to keeping the Sabbath holy (including any kind of work like a woman plucking out a gray hair, deemed a violation). Rather than enhancing the 4th commandment, this *protective hedge* fostered a dull "do's and don'ts" spirituality, the opposite of true faithfulness.

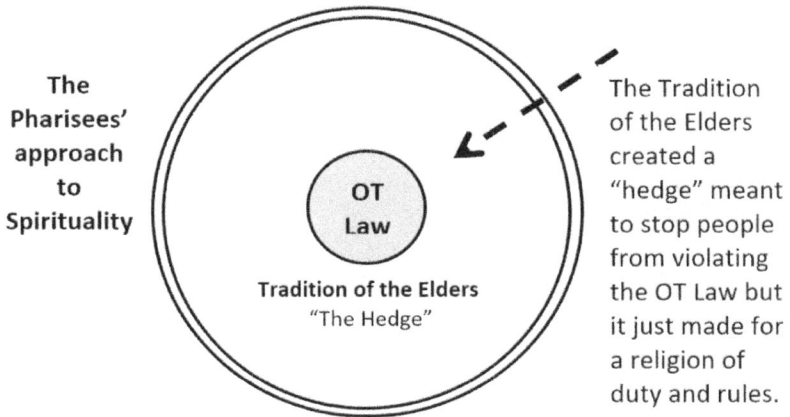

The Pharisees' approach to Spirituality

OT Law

Tradition of the Elders
"The Hedge"

The Tradition of the Elders created a "hedge" meant to stop people from violating the OT Law but it just made for a religion of duty and rules.

Jesus' problem with the Pharisees' approach to spirituality:
The focus becomes PRIDE in your performance of keeping the rules (laws) and not in the pursuit of humility and trust in God.

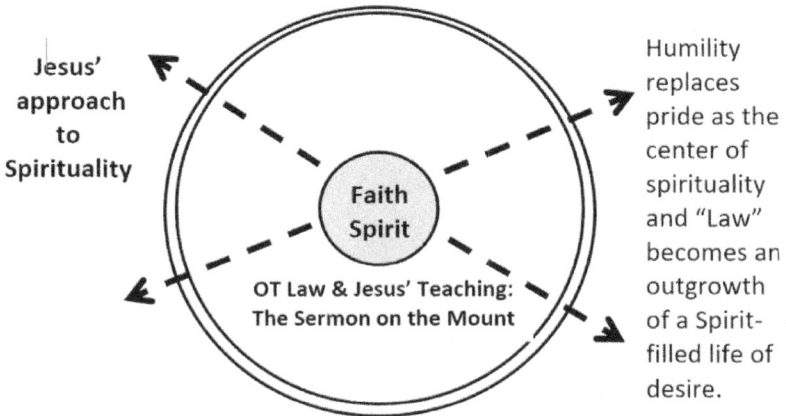

Jesus' approach to Spirituality

Faith
Spirit

OT Law & Jesus' Teaching:
The Sermon on the Mount

Humility replaces pride as the center of spirituality and "Law" becomes an outgrowth of a Spirit-filled life of desire.

Jesus correctly interprets and applies the Old Testament's focus
that TRUST and FAITH in God's performance on our behalf
honors Him and gives us an abundant-filled life.

What were the various Jewish factions?

Pharisees, originating around 150 BC, were
dedicated to the strict observance of Jewish
laws, including oral traditions. Considered
the "gatekeepers" of Judaism, they held
significant influence on the masses.

Sadducees only recognized the Torah and did not accept the validity of
a resurrection or the Pharisees' oral traditions. Mostly wealthy priests
and aristocrats, the Sadducees often held political power.

Herodians were a political faction that backed the Roman-appointed
Herodian dynasty in Judea. They sought to maintain the status quo
under Roman rule and were generally opposed by other Jewish sects.

Zealots, known for their adamant opposition to Roman authorities,
paganism, and polytheism, believed that God was their only ruler and
Lord. They included an even more violent subgroup called the **Sicarii**.

Essenes formed an apocalyptic Judish sect who originated around 100
BC. Not directly mentioned in the Bible, they may be referred to in
Matthew 19:11-12 and Colossians 2:8, 18 and 23. This sect separated
from society, believing the present evil age was coming to an end. They
composed The Qumran (Dead Sea) scrolls discovered in the late 1940's.

Luke 10:38-42 – Martha and Mary

- The village where they live, Bethany, was two miles outside Jerusalem
  (see map on page 178). Martha appears older and acts as the head
  of this sister-led household, which includes their brother, Lazarus.
  Hence, she takes on responsibility for hosting Jesus and his disciples.

- We have heard the enemy of the best is the good and this certainly
  shows up in Martha's actions and her attitude toward Mary. *The
  Chosen* does a good job portraying Jesus' acknowledgement of
  Martha's valuable service but, at the same time, showing how it can
  be a distraction to the true priority of "sitting at his feet."

- Lest we forget, Jesus doesn't need us or our service, we need him and
  his service to us. So, we come to him for forgiveness, renewal and
  wisdom. It is from this strength that we take courage and take action.

REALISTIC But REAL? *That's plausible but did it happen?*

Would the disciples have sold various wares to support their ministry? This creative touch is as plausible as Zebedee sharing profits from his olive oil business and Joanna supporting Jesus' ministry (see Luke 8:3).

Did the disciples have to tote the armor and baggage of Roman soldiers? Very possibly. At least that's the implication and application of Jesus' Sermon on the Mount (Matthew 5:39-41). Here again, we see Jesus showing, not just telling, what it means to follow the Messiah.

Once at Bethany, did the disciples share in the household chores? *The Chosen* closely follows the biblical account of the Mary and Martha dynamics (Luke 10:38-42). But the film has Lazarus and Peter step up to serve the rest of the earthly food while Martha joins the group for the spiritual food that lasts (a nod to Matthew 4:4; Deuteronomy 8:3).

Did Judas have any co-conspirators? Scripture is silent on whether he had a mentor such as Hadad to stir him up. The gospels indicate only that the chief priests (Matthew 26:14-16) and Satan (John 13:27) played a role in Judas' betrayal. This threefold source of temptation is often called "the world, the flesh, and the Devil" (Ephesians 2:2-3).

In Jesus' day, was "resurrection" a metaphor for national renewal? or a physical reality of life after death? The meaning of resurrection was debated then (among the Sadducees and Pharisees), much as it is now. Pharisees believed in a bodily resurrection (Acts 23:6), whereas the Sadducees (*sad-you-see*) did not (Matthew 22:23). The film portrays this debate creatively, involving Yussif, Gederah, Lahad, and Shmuel— all fictional characters who serve a purpose leading up to Jesus' arrest.

We see more of Jesus' mother in the film than we do in Scripture. Was she there all along the way? Scripture indicates Mary's presence only at his birth (Matthew 1:16-25; Luke 1:27-56; 2:1-40), at the temple (Luke 2:41-52), at the wedding in Cana (John 2:1-5), questioning his sanity with other family members (Mark 3:21), at the cross (John 19:25-27), and with the disciples after the Ascension (Acts 1:14). *The Chosen* presumes she was among Jesus' followers all along and fills in gaps with wonderfully poignant conversations.

Drive it Home | Review and Respond: Worship, Pray, Share

Review the study. Watch, listen and sing along with the worship videos.

I Speak Jesus –*Charity Gayle*
Type in URL: tinyurl.com/I-speak-Jesus (7:46 min.)

He Reigns –*Newsboys*
Type in URL: tinyurl.com/he-reigns-song (4:16 min.)

Meditate on Jesus' words in Matthew 5:38-42: *"You have heard it said, 'An eye for an eye and a tooth for a tooth.' But I say to you, Do not resist the one who is evil. But if anyone slaps you on the right cheek, turn to him the other also. And if anyone would sue you and take your tunic, let him have your cloak as well. And if anyone forces you to go one mile, go with him two miles. Give to the one who begs from you, and do not refuse the one who would borrow from you."*

10. Note, in The Chosen, the difference between Jesus' and Judas' mentality toward the Roman conscription. *When, and about what, have you recently felt that life is "unfair"?*

11. *How do you react when life seems unfair?*

… In what ways do Jesus' instructions challenge you?

Video Insights *Should I Follow Tradition?* –Martin Bender
Type in URL: tinyurl.com/should-I-follow-tradition (6:36 min.)
Thoughts:

The Distraction Dilemma –Samer Massad
Type in URL: tinyurl.com/distraction-dilemma (2:53)
Thoughts:

First Things First –Alistair Begg
Type in URL: tinyurl.com/first-things-first-Begg (39:06)
Thoughts:

A. C. T. S. Prayer:

Adoration / Confession / Thanksgiving / Supplication / Steps

Examine where you are with the Lord and the priority of his kingdom. Take it to him in prayer:

ADORATION: How can you praise God from whom all blessings flow?

CONFESSION: What do you need to confess and change?

THANKSGIVING: Which circumstances will you thankfully embrace?

SUPPLICATION: For whom and for what will you pray?

Next STEPS: What will you do with what you've learned? With whom?

PRIOR **to** **STUDY**

Reminder

NOTE FOR LEADERS: Again, **one way to start** the study is to ask group members what is something that they valued or learned from the previous week's ***Drive it Home*** segment after the study.

Dedication (Episode 6)

Study #7

FROM The **CHOSEN**

INTRO: As the Jewish leaders become more serious about eliminating Jesus, the disciples celebrate Hanukkah. Jesus, who is aware of what's coming, struggles with the inability of his disciples to understand.

Hanukkah celebrates the time when the Jews, led by Judah the Maccabee in 139 BC, revolted against the Syrian Greeks, who had desecrated the temple. Many of the Jews expected the Messiah to lead a similar revolt against the Romans. **As you watch, pay particular attention to the growing conflict between Judas and the rest of Jesus' disciples.**

WATCH View Episode 6A (38 ½ min., .20–38:53) > **Discuss**

1. *After watching the Hanukkah celebration, why were many Jews (including Judas) hoping Jesus would do something similar?*

2. *What have you learned so far about comparisons between the kingdom of Jesus and the kingdom of the Maccabees?*

DISCOVER Read > Mark > Discuss **RELATE**

INTRO: At the end of this video section, Jesus tells Judas, "I have sheep and shepherds on my mind." Here, Jesus uses shepherd imagery to compare himself with the religious leaders. He claimed to be the good shepherd and insisted that they were only hired hands.

FROM *The* **BIBLE**

Look for the claims Jesus makes about himself and the accusations he makes against the religious establishment.

I Am the Good Shepherd
JOHN 10 "Truly, truly, I say to you, he who does not enter the sheep-fold by the door but climbs in by another way, that man is a thief and a robber. ² But he who enters by the door is the shepherd of the sheep. ³ To him the gatekeeper opens.

The sheep hear his voice, and he calls his own sheep by name and leads them out. ⁴ When he has brought out all his own, he goes before them, and the sheep follow him, for they know his voice. ⁵ A stranger they will not follow, but they will flee from him, for they do not know the voice of strangers." **⁶** This figure of speech Jesus used with them, but they did not understand what he was saying to them.

⁷ So Jesus again said to them, "Truly, truly, I say to you, I am the door of the sheep. **⁸** All who came before me are thieves and robbers, but the sheep did not listen to them. **⁹** I am the door. If anyone enters by me, he will be saved and will go in and out and find pasture. **¹⁰** The thief comes only to steal and kill and destroy. I came that they may have life and have it abundantly.

¹¹ I am the good shepherd. The good shepherd lays down his life for the sheep. **¹²** He who is a hired hand and not a shepherd, who does not own the sheep, sees the wolf coming and leaves the sheep and flees, and the wolf snatches them and scatters them. **¹³** He flees because he is a hired hand and cares nothing for the sheep. **¹⁴** I am the good shepherd. I know my own and my own know me, **¹⁵** just as the Father knows me and I know the Father; and I lay down my life for the sheep. **¹⁶** And I have other sheep that are not of this fold. I must bring them also, and they will listen to my voice. So there will be one flock, one shepherd.

¹⁷ For this reason the Father loves me, because I lay down my life that I may take it up again. **¹⁸** No one takes it from me, but I lay it down of my own accord. I have authority to lay it down, and I have authority to take it up again. This charge I have received from my Father."

¹⁹ There was again a division among the Jews because of these words. **²⁰** Many of them said, "He has a demon, and is insane; why listen to him?" **²¹** Others said, "These are not the words of one who is oppressed by a demon. Can a demon open the eyes of the blind?"

3. *How does Jesus claim to be like a good shepherd?*

4. *Who is Jesus referring to as "thieves and robbers" and what have they done to the sheep?*

5. *Who are the hired hands and why don't they make good shepherds?*

6. *In verses 17-18, who does Jesus' claim will be responsible for his death?*

WATCH View Episode 6B *(16 min., 38:53 to 55:00)* > **Discuss**

INTRO: Jesus returns to Jerusalem preaching about the Jewish leaders' failure as shepherds, his role as the true shepherd, and his relationship to the Father.

FROM The CHOSEN

DISCOVER Read > Mark > Discuss RELATE

INTRO: The Jewish religious leaders continue to ask Jesus if he is the Messiah, not because they want to know, but because they want evidence to accuse him of a crime.

FROM The BIBLE

Look for Jesus' claims and the Pharisees' accusations.

I and the Father Are One

JOHN 10 ²²At that time the Feast of Dedication took place at Jerusalem. It was winter, ²³ and Jesus was walking in the temple, in the colonnade of Solomon. ²⁴ So the Jews gathered around him and said to him, "How long will you keep us in suspense? If you are the Christ, tell us plainly." ²⁵ Jesus answered them, "I told you, and you do not believe. The works that I do in my Father's name bear witness about me, ²⁶ but you do not believe because you are not among my sheep. ²⁷ My sheep hear my voice, and I know them, and they follow me. ²⁸ I give them eternal life, and they will never perish, and no one will snatch them out of my hand. ²⁹ My Father, who has given them to me, is greater than all, and no one is able to snatch them out of the Father's hand. ³⁰ I and the Father are one."

³¹ The Jews picked up stones again to stone him.

³² Jesus answered them, "I have shown you many good works from the Father; for which of them are you going to stone me?"

³³ The Jews answered him, "It is not for a good work that we are going to stone you but for blasphemy, because you, being a man, make yourself God."

³⁴ Jesus answered them, "Is it not written in your Law, 'I said, you are gods'? ³⁵ If he called them gods to whom the word of God came—and Scripture cannot be broken— ³⁶ do you say of him whom the Father consecrated and sent into the world, 'You are blaspheming,' because I said, 'I am the Son of God'? ³⁷ If I am not doing the works of my Father, then do not believe me; ³⁸ but if I do them, even though you do not believe me, believe the works, that you may know and understand

that the Father is in me and I am in the Father." [39] Again they sought to arrest him, but he escaped from their hands.

7. *What proof does Jesus give the religious leaders that he is the Christ?*

8. *From Jesus' answers to his accusers, what can you conclude that it means to be the Christ (the Messiah)?*

9. *Why don't the religious leaders believe Jesus?*

WATCH **View Episode 6C** *(6 min., 55:00 to 1:01:15)* **> Discuss**

Jesus and the disciples receive news of the death of Lazarus, but the disciples are confused because Jesus had insisted that his sickness would not end in death. Now he says that Lazarus has "fallen asleep" and that he is going to waken him. He wants to give them firmer grounds for belief, so they head back to Bethany, near Jerusalem.

FROM **The CHOSEN**

DISCOVER **Read > Mark > Discuss** **RELATE**

INTRO: Jesus' plans to remain where he was while Lazarus was sick and then to go back to Judea when he died made little sense to his disciples.

FROM **The BIBLE**

Look for his reasons as you study John 11:1-16.

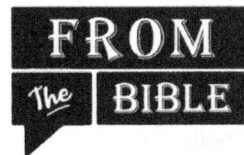

The Death of Lazarus
JOHN 11 Now a certain man was ill, Lazarus of Bethany, the village of Mary and her sister Martha. [2] It was Mary who anointed the Lord with ointment and wiped his feet with her hair, whose brother Lazarus was ill. [3] So the sisters sent to him, saying, "Lord, he whom you love is ill."

[4] But when Jesus heard it he said, "This illness does not lead to death. It is for the glory of God, so that the Son of God may be glorified through it."

[5] Now Jesus loved Martha and her sister and Lazarus. [6] So, when he heard that Lazarus was ill, he stayed two days longer in the place where he was. [7] Then after this he said to the disciples, "Let us go to Judea again."

[8] The disciples said to him, "Rabbi, the Jews were just now seeking to stone you, and are you going there again?"

[9] Jesus answered, "Are there not twelve hours in the day? If anyone walks in the day, he does not stumble, because he sees the light of this world. [10] But if anyone walks in the night, he stumbles, because the light is not in him." [11] After saying these things, he said to them, "Our friend Lazarus has fallen asleep, but I go to awaken him."

[12] The disciples said to him, "Lord, if he has fallen asleep, he will recover." [13] Now Jesus had spoken of his death, but they thought that he meant taking rest in sleep.

[14] Then Jesus told them plainly, "Lazarus has died, [15] and for your sake I am glad that I was not there, so that you may believe. But let us go to him."

16 So Thomas, called the Twin, said to his fellow disciples, "Let us also go, that we may die with him."

10. *What legitimate safety reasons would Jesus and the disciples have for not going to Judea?*

... Why does he insist on going?

11. *What does Jesus want his disciples to know about light and dark, day and night?*

12. *What answers and encouragements do they offer to each other?*

... How does Thomas' statement summarize the situation?

T-Shirt Design After watching > discovering > relating,
What slogan would you write or draw on your T-Shirt?

Draft concepts:

Final design:

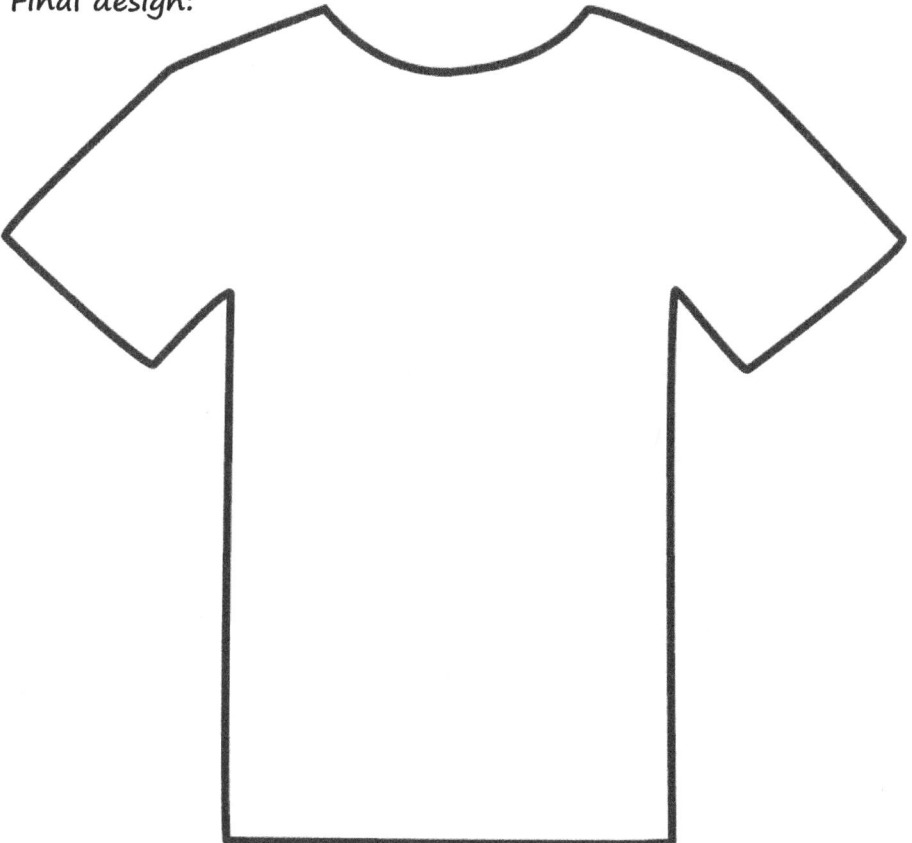

NOTES on Study #7 *Commentary and Historical Context*

John 10:1-21 – I Am the Good Shepherd
- In the OT, a shepherd symbolized a royal caretaker or leader of God's people. God was the "Shepherd of Israel" (Psalm 80:1) and behaved accordingly (Psalm 23; Isaiah 40:10-11; Ezekiel 34:11-16). God exposed false shepherds or watchmen (Isaiah 56:9-12; Ezekiel 34) and promised that a true Shepherd, the Messiah, would come.

- Several flocks under one watchman were confined behind gated walls. Their respective shepherd would lead out those sheep who knew his voice. The shepherd led from in front, not driving the flock from behind. By contrast, the hired hand would break in to steal and destroy, or abandon them to predators, as he cared only for wages, not sheep. Jesus likens himself to the "gate" and "good shepherd."

- A shepherd of ancient Palestine might take risks to protect his sheep, but not at the risk of losing his life. By contrast, Jesus will die for his sheep. This ultimate loyalty also extends to "other sheep"—to those outside Judaism, that is, the worldwide scope of the Church.

John 10:22-39 – I and the Father Are One
- The Feast of Dedication, also known as Hanukkah, commemorates the revolt by Judas Maccabeus revolt from 167-160 BC to restore the Temple after being profaned by Antiochus Epiphanes. Many awaited "the Christ" (Greek for Messiah) to lead another such deliverance.

- Knowing that he was the Christ, but would not fulfill their Messianic expectations, Jesus points to his works and his union with God the Father. This latter claim was blasphemous to the Jewish leaders.

John 11:1-16 – The Death of Lazarus
- This was not a case of "sickness unto death" nor of "falling asleep" (a euphemism for death); this was an occasion for God to be glorified by another miracle, as in the case of the man born blind. (9:3; 11:4).

- The two days that Jesus stays behind (11:6), plus one day for the messengers to arrive from Bethany and one day for Jesus to return with them equals "four days" (11:17,39). The soul was thought to hover near the body for three days, in the hope of returning to it. Hence, in four days all such hope is lost; Lazarus is irrevocably dead.

The "I Am" Statements of Jesus

The phrase "I am" first appears in Exodus 3:13-15, where God reveals himself to Moses as "I AM WHO I AM." The metaphorical "I Am" statements of Jesus, which appear only in the Gospel of John, are a series of declarations made by Jesus, to highlight different aspects of his divine character and mission. Each statement reflects his nature like unto God and reveals how Jesus fulfills our spiritual needs.

The nine "I am" sayings recorded in John are shown in this wheel as nine categories and one center point. Note that one "I am" saying (John 14:6: the way, truth, life) is a kind of three-in-one. The radical claim to pre-existence and God's very name (8:58; "Before Abraham was born, I am") is the central point and is thus shown here as the hub.

The meaning of each "spoke" is explored, contextually, in the notes for each study. In application, we will encounter Jesus as the *Bread of Life* to sustain us (6:35), the *Light of the World* to guide and convict us (8:12), the *Gate and Good Shepherd* of the sheep to protect and to guide us (10:7, 11), and as the *Resurrection* to give us life eternal (11:25). Thus, we know Jesus as the *Way*, the *Truth*, and the *Life* (14:6). All of which makes him the *Real Vine* (15:1), connecting us to God as his sons and daughters.

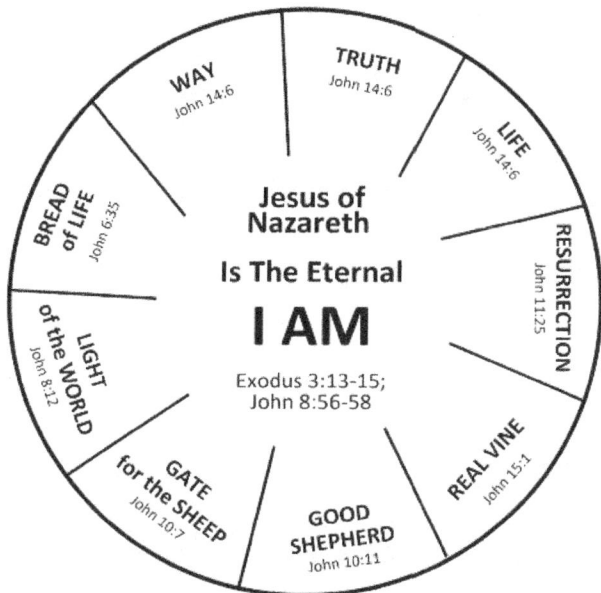

The graph and its importance in the Gospel of John is also referenced on page 171.

REALISTIC But REAL?

That's plausible but did it happen?

Did Jesus celebrate Hanukkah? Likely. Hanukkah is not mentioned in Scripture, per se but Jesus' presence and triumph of light over darkness is associated with that event aka the "Feast of Dedication" (John 10:22).

Is the Hanukkah celebration accurate? Yes. In *The Chosen,* Jesus' disciples do a playful re-enactment of the horrific and heroic events that Hanukkah celebrates, dating back to 156 B.C. For biblical prophecy of these events, see Daniel 11; for historical detail, see the apocryphal Book of First Maccabees. The joyous singing of Psalms 113, 116, and 118, along with Miriam's song in Exodus 15, are also biblical traditions.

The lighting of the traditional eight candles memorializes the time when the lamp oil in the temple miraculously kept the light on for eight days instead of just one. The disciples' joyful mood portrayed in *The Chosen* serves to counterbalance the gloom that looms for one and all.

For dramatic effect, it's hard to beat the stone-pelted disciples fleeing for their lives—but did that happen? It could have but is not recorded in Scripture. Likely, no one could remain neutral after Jesus' Good Shepherd speech (John 10:1-21). All of this sets up the group to receive another blow: Lazarus is dead. Then more bad news: Religious leaders plot to have Jesus executed. Interestingly, Jesus and his disciples are in Bethany (east of the Jordon River) when they receive the news and now must go to Bethany (west of the Jordan River). See map on page 178.

Did Jesus really mock and laugh derisively at the Pharisees? This fiery denunciation of religious leaders by Jesus, as highlighted in this film and recorded in Matthew 23, is the real Jesus. He is rightly concerned with genuine righteousness and disdains religious hypocrisy.

Why did Thomas want to die with Lazarus? In Scripture (John 11:16), Thomas appears brave in his declaration, whereas in *The Chosen,* that line stems from his depression and a possible death wish.

That sheep automatically follows the voice of their Shepherd, and that some people are healed whereas others are not—is that a result of human choice or God's will, as the analogy applies to us?

The film, as does Scripture, leaves us to ponder the tension between God's foreknowledge, God's will, and human agency (free will). Being an ecumenical project, *The Chosen* wisely avoids taking a position in this classic debate and simply affirms that both viewpoints matter. This is part of why it's difficult for the disciples of Jesus, then and now, to make sense of life's chaotic events!

Drive it Home Review and Respond: Worship, Pray, Share

Review John 10:1-30 and examine your own journey of questions, doubts and faith. Again, consider how the Shepherd-Sheep imagery relates to you. **Look for everything Jesus says about sheep.**

- They hear the shepherd's voice, verse 3
- They are called by name, verse 3
- They know the shepherd's voice, verse 4
- They follow the shepherd, verse 4
- They flee from strangers, verse 5
- They will enter the sheepfold by the door (who is Jesus), verse 9
- They find pasture, verse 9
- They know the shepherd, verse 14
- They are part of one flock, verse 16
- They are given eternal life, verse 28
- They cannot be snatched away from their shepherd, verse 28

The Battle Belongs to You –Phil Wickham
Type in URL: tinyurl.com/battle-belongs (4:45 min.)

The Way –Pat Barrett
Type in URL: tinyurl.com/the-way-song (4:19 min.)

13. *From the description Jesus gives in John 10, do you consider yourself to be one of his sheep? If not (and if so) what does this mean to you?*

Video Insights My Sheep Hear My Voice *-P.J. Stephen Paul*
Type in URL: tinyurl.com/Shepherd-voice (1:09 min.)
Thoughts:

One Door, One Shepherd, One Flock *-Alistair Begg*
Type in URL: tinyurl.com/one-door-one-shepherd (41:03 min.)
Thoughts: (25:50 min.)

John 10:22-42 Bible Study with Me *-Michael Hoff*
Type in URL: tinyurl.com/john-10-bible-study (8:56)
Thoughts:

A. C. T. S. Prayer:
Adoration / Confession / Thanksgiving / Supplication / Steps

Examine where you are with the Lord and the priority of his kingdom. Take it to him in prayer:

ADORATION: How can you praise God from whom all blessings flow?

CONFESSION: What do you need to confess and change?

THANKSGIVING: Which circumstances will you thankfully embrace?

SUPPLICATION: For whom and for what will you pray?

Next STEPS: What will you do with what you've learned? With whom?

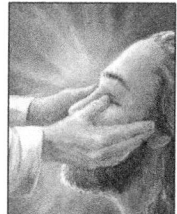

PRIOR To STUDY

What is your favorite Chosen scene so far?

NOTE FOR EVERYONE: Of course, there's a wide difference of opinion regarding the above question, but many may pick one from this episode. At some point it would prove fun to take a vote... and then to have group members describe why they chose the one they did.

The Last Sign (Episode 7)

Study #8

FROM The **CHOSEN**

INTRO: The episode begins in the future with a visit from old friends, Matthew and Mary Magdalene. They have much to talk about. Likewise, when the episode shifts back to the present, with the disciples heading back to Bethany and Lazarus' tomb, they have much to talk about. Their present conversation centers around the future—that is, what they fear might come next.

WATCH | View Episode 7A *(46 ½ min., .20 to 46:58)* > **Discuss**

INTRO: As you watch the first part of Episode 7, think about the questions and problems faced by each character as they face the reality of Lazarus' death... and his resurrection.

MAN RISES FROM THE DEAD! Shouldn't this headline cause universal joy and excitement? Unfortunately, not in Bethany of Judea. Instead of bringing people together, Lazarus' raising caused even more division. **Be sure to notice each character's reactions to this miraculous event.**

1. *What questions do the disciples raise?*

2. *What answers do they receive?*

DISCOVER Read > Mark > Discuss **RELATE**

INTRO: The story of Lazarus rising from the dead is found below in John 11:17-44.

FROM *The* **BIBLE**

Look for and identify the characters and their reactions to Jesus as you study this passage.

I Am the Resurrection and the Life
JOHN 11 ¹⁷ Now when Jesus came, he found that Lazarus had already been in the tomb four days. ¹⁸ Bethany was near Jerusalem, about two miles off, ¹⁹ and many of the Jews had come to Martha and Mary to console them concerning their brother.

²⁰ So when Martha heard that Jesus was coming, she went and met him, but Mary remained seated in the house. ²¹ Martha said to Jesus, "Lord, if you had been here, my brother would not have died. ²² But even now I know that whatever you ask from God, God will give you."

[23] Jesus said to her, "Your brother will rise again." [24] Martha said to him, "I know that he will rise again in the resurrection on the last day."

[25] Jesus said to her, "I am the resurrection and the life. Whoever believes in me, though he die, yet shall he live, [26] and everyone who lives and believes in me shall never die. Do you believe this?"

[27] She said to him, "Yes, Lord; I believe that you are the Christ, the Son of God, who is coming into the world."

Jesus Weeps

[28] When she had said this, she went and called her sister Mary, saying in private, "The Teacher is here and is calling for you." [29] And when she heard it, she rose quickly and went to him.

[30] Now Jesus had not yet come into the village, but was still in the place where Martha had met him. [31] When the Jews who were with her in the house, consoling her, saw Mary rise quickly and go out, they followed her, supposing that she was going to the tomb to weep there.

[32] Now when Mary came to where Jesus was and saw him, she fell at his feet, saying to him, "Lord, if you had been here, my brother would not have died."

[33] When Jesus saw her weeping, and the Jews who had come with her also weeping, he was deeply moved in his spirit and greatly troubled.

[34] And he said, "Where have you laid him?"

They said to him, "Lord, come and see."

[35] Jesus wept.

[36] So the Jews said, "See how he loved him!" [37] But some of them said, "Could not he who opened the eyes of the blind man also have kept this man from dying?"

Jesus Raises Lazarus

[38] Then Jesus, deeply moved again, came to the tomb. It was a cave, and a stone lay against it. [39] Jesus said, "Take away the stone."

Martha, the sister of the dead man, said to him, "Lord, by this time there will be an odor, for he has been dead four days."

[40] Jesus said to her, "Did I not tell you that if you believed you would see the glory of God?" [41] So they took away the stone. And Jesus lifted up his eyes and said, "Father, I thank you that you have heard me. [42] I knew that you always hear me, but I said this on account of the people standing around, that they may believe that you sent me." [43] When he had said these things, he cried out with a loud voice, "Lazarus, come out." [44] The man who had died came out, his hands and feet bound with linen strips, and his face wrapped with a cloth. Jesus said to them, "Unbind him, and let him go."

3. In verse 27, Martha confesses, "I believe that you are the Christ, the Son of God, who is coming into the world." *To what extent do you think she understood what she said?*

4. *Why did Jesus weep (v. 35), and why was he "deeply moved" (v. 38)?*

5. *Why did Jesus raise Lazarus from the dead?*

WATCH View Episode 7B (11 min., 46:58 to 57:37) > **Discuss**

INTRO: What would you ask a previously dead person (and we're not talking about someone who wrote a book about returning from death, we're talking about an actual previously dead person)? Likely we'd all ask the same question Mary asks Lazarus, *"What was it like?"*

Jesus said that the raising of Lazarus was a sign; however, it was a sign that many either didn't see, misread, or were threatened by. Even Lazarus had difficulty understanding. In her writings, Mary communicates such foreboding to Matthew at the end of the episode.

DISCOVER Read > Mark > Discuss **RELATE**

INTRO: Lazarus too was confused especially why Jesus spoke about dying until Jesus explained it in the light of Isaiah 53, a prophecy written 700 years earlier. The prophecy explains the nature of the Messiah being that of a *Suffering Servant*.

FROM *The* **BIBLE**

Look for comparisons between the Suffering Servant and what you know about Jesus from *Scripture* and *The Chosen*.

Surely He Has Borne Our Griefs
ISAIAH 53 Who has believed what he has heard from us?

And to whom has the arm of the LORD been revealed?

² For he grew up before him like a young plant,

and like a root out of dry ground;

he had no form or majesty that we should look at him,

and no beauty that we should desire him.

³ **He was despised and rejected by men,**

a man of sorrows and acquainted with grief;

and as one from whom men hide their faces

he was despised, and we esteemed him not.

> [4] Surely he has borne our griefs
>
>   and carried our sorrows;
>
> yet we esteemed him stricken,
>
>   smitten by God, and afflicted.
>
> [5] But he was pierced for our transgressions;
>
>   he was crushed for our iniquities;
>
> upon him was the chastisement that brought us peace,
>
>   and with his wounds we are healed.
>
> [6] All we like sheep have gone astray;
>
>   we have turned—every one—to his own way;
>
> and the LORD has laid on him
>
>   the iniquity of us all.

6. *What does this prophecy say will happen to the Suffering Servant?*

7. *What do you find surprising or disturbing about this prophecy?*

8. *What evidence do you find that this prophecy is speaking about Jesus?*

WATCH   *View Episode 7C* (13 min., 57:37 to 1:10:05) **> Discuss**

INTRO: The disciples are quite confused about what the "biggest public sign" of Jesus means or where it leads for him—and for them.

The episode ends where it started with Mary and Matthew talking in retrospect about these events. Mary then reads her journal thoughts to Matthew which seems to sum up their dilemma and ours. **After watching the end of this episode, feel free to end with her reading:**

"Darkness is not the absence of light, that would be too simple. It's more uncontrollable and sinister. Not a place, but a void. I was there once. More than once. And, although I could not see or hear you, you were there, waiting. Because the darkness is not dark to you, at least it's not always.

You wept, not because your friend was dead, but because soon you would be, and because we couldn't understand it. Or didn't want to, or both. The coming darkness was too deep for us to grasp. But then so is the light. One had to come before the other. It was always that way with you. It still is.

Tears fell from your eyes, and then ours, before every light in the world went out. And time itself wanted to die with you. I go back to that place sometimes. Or rather, it comes back to me, uninvited.

The night, it was eternal, until it wasn't. Bitter, and then sweet. Some-how the bitter remained in the sweet and has never gone away. You told us it would be like that, not with your words, but with how you lived: **The man of sorrows, acquainted with grief.** *That grief wasn't what we wanted to see, so we tried to look away. And in so doing, fulfilled your very essence:* **One from whom people hide their faces.**

But soon we couldn't hide from it any more than we could stop the sun from setting or rising. I remember you wishing there could be another way, and looking back, I do too. I still don't know why it has to be this way, the bitter, often mingled with the sweet. Maybe I never will, at least not this side of. . . .   –Mary Magdalene, in *The Chosen*

T-Shirt Design After watching > discovering > relating, What slogan would you write or draw on your T-Shirt?

Draft concepts:

Final design:

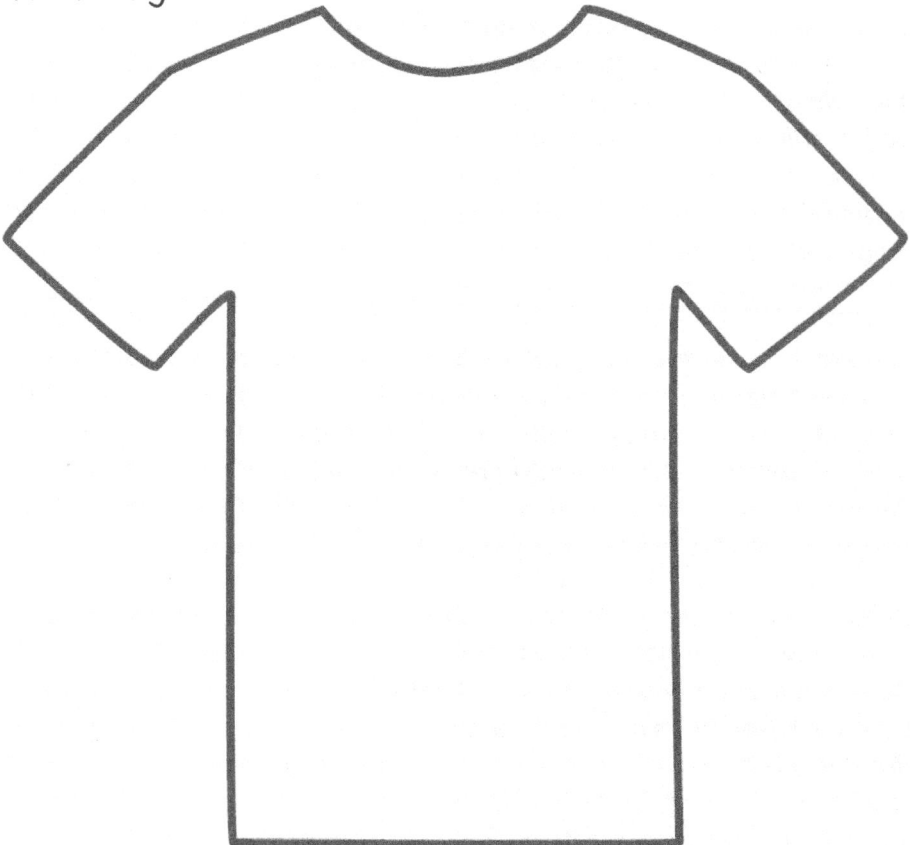

NOTES on Study #8 *Commentary and Historical Context*

John 11:17-44 – I Am the Resurrection and the Life

- Jesus is greeted as "Lord" (11:21,32,34), "The Teacher" (11:28), "the Christ" and "Son of God" (11:27). He truly mourns (11:33-36) as befits a funeral; he "wept" (shed tears), as distinct from "wailing" (loud grief of professional mourners). But Jesus jars everyone when he says he is the source of resurrected life (11:23-26)!

- Martha believes in a resurrection, generally (11:24), as did the Pharisees. Martha also believes, more specifically, that Jesus can and will deliver on this promise (11:25-27) as a healer. Yet she will be surprised by Jesus raising a man who's been dead for four days (11:39-40). Jesus confronts her with the fact that he is Lord of life.

  Martha's likely younger sister, Mary, mirrors her consternation that Jesus didn't come sooner to cure her brother rather than allowing him to die. (They both agonize over the age-old question of why God does what he does in human affairs, and Jesus, by his explanation and actions, conveys the answer: God's purposes are often beyond our capability to understand them.)

- Jesus' tears are not for their loss since he knows what is about to happen, but for the human toll of sin, disease, and death.

- A tomb carved out of a cave, with a stone that rolls away, indicates a person of wealth or importance. That Lazarus has been dead for four days indicates significant decomposition, in contrast to others Jesus has raised to this point (Matthew 11:5; Mark 5:22-43; Luke 7:11-15).

Isaiah 53:1-6 – Surely He Has Borne Our Griefs

- Jesus came from humble roots, but with no beauty or majesty as did David; rather, he was rejected by his people (John 1:10-11).

- Jesus suffered not for anything he did but was afflicted with the infirmities of others, of each of us.

- "Pierced" and "crushed" refer to the physical and emotional agony of carrying those undeserved sins and the spiritual angst of being separated from his Father, God—not just of dying in itself. The result is peace, healing, and forgiveness for sinners (1 Peter 2:24).

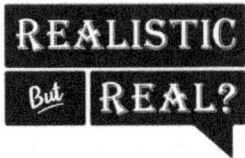

REALISTIC But REAL? **Was there a "Gospel according to Mary Magdalene"?** Yes, however, it did not make it into the Bible. Several pages of this original manuscript are lost. What remains is of interest but does not meet the criteria to be included in the canonical gospels. Many, including *The Chosen*, have attempted to reconstruct what is missing from Mary's bittersweet poem about good and evil. We like their version! Here's the original: thegospelofmary.org/the-gospel

Did 'Little James' meet a tragic end as a martyr? Yes, as did most of the Twelve, but how and when remains an open question. One tradition holds that he was beheaded, another that he was stoned to death. In *The Chosen*, he is said to have been speared by a sword.

Was Lazarus dead? or just asleep? Dead, by all accounts. Jesus' metaphor of likening death to sleep (John 11:11-14; compare Psalm 13:3) confused some disciples. Hence, he waited the extra two days to raise Lazarus, in part, to convince everyone that Lazarus really was dead and not just resuscitated from a swoon or revived from a coma-like slumber. Raising Lazarus prefigures what will happen to Jesus after he dies.

Did the events surrounding the raising of Lazarus happen as depicted in *The Chosen*? Yes, the film closely follows John's Gospel (11:17-44). The film adds the presence of Jesus' mother to comfort him,... the confusion, grief, and anger of Thomas,... the mix of shock, joy, and concern shared by the reunited Lazarus, Mary, Martha, and others,... the presence of Adnan (identified as Yussif's father) who will offer follow-up care,... plus all the table talk to process what just happened, including a discussion with a disoriented Lazarus. Surely, much of this happened!

Did Jesus have a sense of humor? Yes. See, for example, his sarcasm on display in Matthew 11:7-10 about John the Baptist. Leave it to *The Chosen* to develop further this endearing aspect of Jesus.

Given Mary Magdalene's relapses and flashbacks, was she "delivered" of demons—or not? The biblical record indicates only that she once had seven demons (Luke 8:3), but does not fill in the gaps, before or after her spiritual deliverance. *The Chosen* plausibly portrays the oppressive dark times that are normative for such troubled souls.

Drive it Home | Review and Respond: Worship, Pray, Share

Go back through the study, especially Lazarus' resurrection. Listen and sing along with this worship song.

Living Hope –Phil Wickham
Type in URL: tinyurl.com/living-hope-worship (5:31 min.)

Man of Sorrows –Hillsong
Type in URL: tinyurl.com/man-of-sorrows (5:19 min.)

Take time to meditate on Psalm 13:

> How long, O Lord? Will you forget me forever?
>   How long will you hide your face from me?
> ² How long must I take counsel in my soul
>   and have sorrow in my heart all the day?
> How long shall my enemy be exalted over me?
> ³ Consider and answer me, O Lord my God;
>   light up my eyes, lest I sleep the sleep of death,
> ⁴ lest my enemy say, "I have prevailed over him,"
>   lest my foes rejoice because I am shaken.
> ⁵ But I have trusted in your steadfast love;
>   my heart shall rejoice in your salvation.
> ⁶ I will sing to the Lord,
>   because he has dealt bountifully with me.

8. With which lines of this Psalm are you able to identify?

9. If light of the hope of the Resurrection, what do verses 5-6 mean for you?

Video Insights The Raising of Lazarus in John 11 –Chad Bird
Type in URL: https://tinyurl.com/Lazarus-raised (35:42 min)
Thoughts:
_____

Jesus Wept –Steven Curtis Chapman
Type in URL: tinyurl.com/Jesus-Wept-John-11 (3:04 min.)
Thoughts:
_____

Imputation: Sermon on Isaiah 53:6 –Colin Smith
Type in URL: tinyurl.com/Imputation-Isaiah-53 (37:42 min)
Thoughts:
_____

A. C. T. S. Prayer:
Adoration / Confession / Thanksgiving / Supplication / Steps

Examine where you are with the Lord and the priority of his kingdom. Take it to him in prayer:

ADORATION: How can you praise God from whom all blessings flow?

CONFESSION: What do you need to confess and change?

THANKSGIVING: Which circumstances will you thankfully embrace?

SUPPLICATION: For whom and for what will you pray?

Next STEPS: What will you do with what you've learned? With whom?

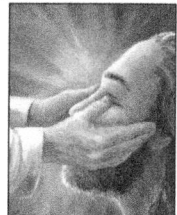

PRIOR to STUDY

A Possible 11th Study: Pages 160-168

NOTE FOR LEADERS: Upcoming is the 9th study and there is one more... or maybe two if you'd like! You could plan for an *11th Study Overview and Wrap-Up*. Here are three options:

1) Your group could meet at its **normal time and do its usual study**. In this case, you would use pages 160-168 to guide the 11th study called "Your Faith Journey."

2) As an alternative, your group could schedule an **all-day event**,* perhaps a Saturday gathering—maybe at a different location, and extend the "Your Faith Journey" interaction together.

3) Or your group could extend the study further as a **weekend retreat*** to include even more time for study, prayer, quiet time, and fun!

One way or another, think through how to make your last gathering special and a time that provides momentum for your next study!

*For more input on creating longer events, see *Leaders* on the website.

Humble (Episode 8)

Study #9

INTRO: Passover is a defining event for the nation of Israel. It explains how the Jews transitioned from Egyptian slaves to God's chosen people, how they understood redemption, and how they came to a knowledge of God, with their hopes for future salvation.

FROM The **CHOSEN**

WATCH View Episode 8A (3 ½ min., from .20 to 3:43) > **Discuss**

Here King David and Queen Bathsheba are helping their son, Daniel, understand and prepare for the sacrifice of a lamb that will live in their home for five days.

FROM
The CHOSEN

DISCOVER Read Aloud > Mark It Up > Discuss

INTRO: Below are the instructions for the first Passover from the book of Exodus.

Look for the commands and instructions given.

FROM
The BIBLE

The Passover

EXODUS 12 The Lord said to Moses and Aaron in the land of Egypt. . .

[3] Tell all the congregation of Israel that on the tenth day of this month every man shall take a lamb according to their fathers' houses, a lamb for a household. . . . [5] Your lamb shall be without blemish, a male a year old. You may take it from the sheep or from the goats, [6] and you shall keep it until the fourteenth day of this month, when the whole assembly of the congregation of Israel shall kill their lambs at twilight.

[7] "Then they shall take some of the blood and put it on the two door-posts and the lintel of the houses in which they eat it. [8] They shall eat the flesh that night, roasted on the fire; with unleavened bread and bitter herbs they shall eat it. [9] Do not eat any of it raw or boiled in water, but roasted, its head with its legs and its inner parts. [10] And you shall let none of it remain until the morning; anything that remains until the morning you shall burn.

[11] In this manner you shall eat it: with your belt fastened, your sandals on your feet, and your staff in your hand. And you shall eat it in haste. It

is the Lord's Passover. [12] For I will pass through the land of Egypt that night, and I will strike all the firstborn in the land of Egypt, both man and beast; and on all the gods of Egypt I will execute judgments: I am the Lord. [13] The blood shall be a sign for you, on the houses where you are. And when I see the blood, I will pass over you, and no plague will befall you to destroy you, when I strike the land of Egypt. [14] "This day shall be for you a memorial day, and you shall keep it as a feast to the Lord; throughout your generations, as a statute forever, you shall keep it as a feast. [15] Seven days you shall eat unleavened bread.

1. *What are the requirements for choosing a lamb?*

... What are the people to do, and not do, with their lamb?

2. *What is the significance of the lamb and its blood?*

WATCH View Episode 8B (13 ½ min., 4.45 to 18:07) > **Discuss**

INTRO: As Lazarus' sister, Mary, is on her mission to find the best perfume that money can buy, the conflict surrounding Jesus increases. The Roman and Jewish authorities wonder what is happening and how they should respond. Is Jesus a threat? A passing fad? Or nothing to be bothered about? Everyone needs to decide.

FROM The **CHOSEN**

3. *What is the perspective of the Roman authorities concerning... Jesus?*

... the Jewish leaders?

DISCOVER Read Aloud > Mark It Up > Discuss

INTRO: How do powerful people react when they feel threatened? They wield their power. Jesus' popularity, miracles, and message felt like a threat to those who preferred the status quo. Wanting to stay in power, they decided it was time to act. Little did they know, they were acting out a much larger agenda: God's plan of salvation.

FROM The **BIBLE**

As you read this passage, seek to identify who, what, and why.

The Plot to Kill Jesus
JOHN 11 [45] Many of the Jews therefore, who had come with Mary and had seen what he did, believed in him, [46] but some of them went to the Pharisees and told them what Jesus had done. [47] So the chief priests and the Pharisees gathered the council and said, "What are we to do? For this man performs many signs. [48] If we let him go on like this, everyone will believe in him, and the Romans will come and take away both our place and our nation."

[49] But one of them, Caiaphas, who was high priest that year, said to them, "You know nothing at all. [50] Nor do you understand that it is better for you that one man should die for the people, not that the whole nation should perish." [51] He did not say this of his own accord, but being high priest that year he prophesied that Jesus would die for the nation, [52] and not for the nation only, but also to gather into one the children of God who are scattered abroad. [53] So from that day on they made plans to put him to death. [54] Jesus therefore no longer walked openly among the Jews, but went from there to the region near the wilderness, to a town called Ephraim, and there he stayed with the disciples.

[55] Now the Passover of the Jews was at hand, and many went up from the country to Jerusalem before the Passover to purify themselves. [56] They were looking for Jesus and saying to one another as they stood in the temple, "What do you think? That he will not come to the feast at all?" [57] Now the chief priests and the Pharisees had given orders that if anyone knew where he was, he should let them know, so that they might arrest him.

4. *Why were the chief priests and Pharisees concerned about Jesus?*

... What plans did they make?

5. *What double meaning is there to Caiaphas' words?*

6. *How did the plot by the chief priests and Pharisees affect Jesus and his disciples*

WATCH View Episode 8C *(15 min., 18.07 to 32:46)* > **Discuss**

INTRO: As thousands arrive in Jerusalem for the annual Passover celebration, Jesus talks with a representative of the Jewish Sanhedrin, Shumel. Shumel confides in Jesus his view of the Messiah and how he might participate in God's coming kingdom. Jesus then tells him and those present, a parable (and an Old Testament teaching, page 141) that describes what that kingdom is really like.

FROM The **CHOSEN**

DISCOVER Read > Mark > Discuss **RELATE**

INTRO: What is the kingdom of God, and who is included in it? In Matthew 25: 31-46, Jesus tells three parables to answer those questions. We will look at the third of those parables.

FROM The **BIBLE**

Look for the contrasts between the sheep and the goats.

The Final Judgment
MATTHEW 25 [31] "When the Son of Man comes in his glory, and all the angels with him, then he will sit on his glorious throne. [32] Before him will be gathered all the nations, and he will separate people one from another as a shepherd separates the sheep from the goats. [33] And he

will place the sheep on his right, but the goats on the left.

34 Then the King will say to those on his right, 'Come, you who are blessed by my Father, inherit the kingdom prepared for you from the foundation of the world. 35 For I was hungry and you gave me food, I was thirsty and you gave me drink, I was a stranger and you welcomed me, 36 I was naked and you clothed me, I was sick and you visited me, I was in prison and you came to me.'

37 Then the righteous will answer him, saying, 'Lord, when did we see you hungry and feed you, or thirsty and give you drink? 38 And when did we see you a stranger and welcome you, or naked and clothe you? 39 And when did we see you sick or in prison and visit you?'

40 And the King will answer them, 'Truly, I say to you, as you did it to one of the least of these my brothers, you did it to me.'

41 "Then he will say to those on his left, 'Depart from me, you cursed, into the eternal fire prepared for the devil and his angels. 42 For I was hungry and you gave me no food, I was thirsty and you gave me no drink, 43 I was a stranger and you did not welcome me, naked and you did not clothe me, sick and in prison and you did not visit me.'

44 Then they also will answer, saying, 'Lord, when did we see you hungry or thirsty or a stranger or naked or sick or in prison, and did not minister to you?'

45 Then he will answer them, saying, 'Truly, I say to you, as you did not do it to one of the least of these, you did not do it to me.' 46 And these will go away into eternal punishment, but the righteous into eternal life."

8. *In this parable, who is the King, who are the sheep, and who are the goats?*

9. *What is given to the sheep and why?*

10. *What happens to the goats and why?*

11. *According to the parable, where in the world can the King be found?*

... Why is he not usually identified?

DISCOVER Read > Mark > Discuss **RELATE**

INTRO: In this episode Jesus confronts Shumel with the difference between his contemporaries' spiritual values and what God truly values. In doing so he quotes from the Old Testament.

FROM The BIBLE

Look for things valued from this passage.

What Does the Lord Require?

MICAH 6 ⁶ "With what shall I come before the Lord,

and bow myself before God on high?

Shall I come before him with burnt offerings,

with calves a year old?

⁷ Will the Lord be pleased with thousands of rams,

with ten thousands of rivers of oil?

Shall I give my firstborn for my transgression,

the fruit of my body for the sin of my soul?"

⁸ **He has told you, O man, what is good;**

and what does the Lord require of you

but to do justice, and to love kindness,

and to walk humbly with your God.

11. *According to this passage, what did people expect would be pleasing to God?*

... In contrast, what does the Lord value?

T-Shirt Design After watching > discovering > relating, What slogan would you write or draw on your T-Shirt?

Draft concepts:

Final design:

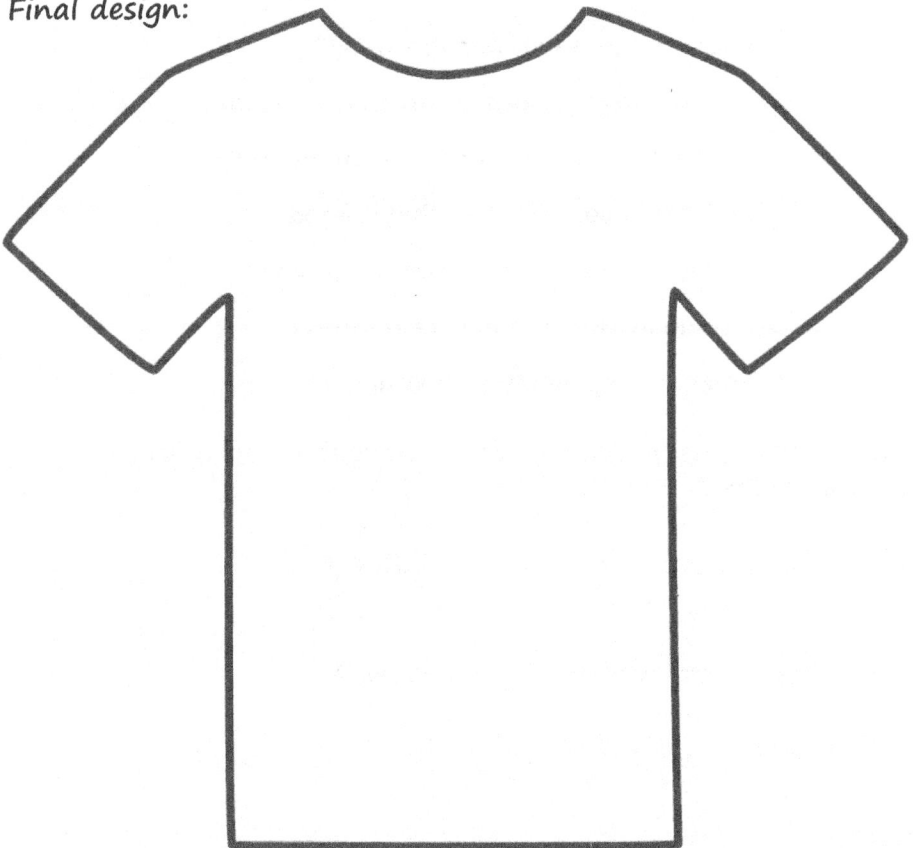

NOTES on Study #9 *Commentary and Historical Context*

Exodus 12:1-15 – The Passover
- The "first month" of Israel's religious new year was meant to remind Israel of their Exodus from slavery in Egypt—their new lease on life.

- A "lamb without defect" was to be sacrificed and eaten, whose blood was then spread on the doorframes of the household.

- The "bitter herbs" (endive, chicory, and other bitter-tasting plants indigenous to Egypt) were to be eaten to remind the Hebrews of their bitter years in servitude.

- Their manner of eating (cloak tucked in... staff in hand) reminded them of their initial exodus in "haste".

- As with the other nine plagues, judgment would be on "all the gods of Egypt"—none of whom could stop the Lord's Passover.

Matthew 25:31-46 – The Final Judgment
- Though there are differing interpretations here, it is likely this passage refers to the Great White Throne judgment at the end of the age (Revelation 20:11-15)—a judgment based on how one treats God's people, and thus ultimately God himself.

  The result for sheep is the eternal enjoyment of God's fellowship, or for goats, suffering the punishment of hell (that is, eternal separation from God).

- As God gives out of grace, his fellowship reward is not based on merit. We do good from a new heart, having experienced being loved by God, not by an empty attempt to earn his love.

Micah 6:6-8 – What Does the Lord Require?
- Micah echoes other prophets (1 Samuel 15:22; Psalm 51:16-17; Isaiah 1:11-17; Hosea 6:6) in prioritizing justice, kindness, and humility over sacrifice, including the important sacrifice visualized in the Passover!

REALISTIC But REAL?

That's plausible but did it happen?

Was "King David riding a donkey" just a literary prologue? Or historically prophetic in getting Jesus ready to re-enter Jerusalem? The royal donkey was like an ancient Air Force One, a sign of kingliness (Zechariah 9:9-10). The one in charge rode on a donkey, not a warhorse as would a military conqueror. Jesus was instead fulfilling Zechariah's prophecy.

David ascended to the throne with hardship; he had no opportunity to parade in Jerusalem. But he did have Solomon ride on his royal donkey, to establish Solomon as the rightful successor to the Davidic kingdom. That move upstaged David's rebel son Adonijah, who was attempting a coup with a private self-coronation complete with the pomp of war-horses (1 Kings 1). Jesus is likewise upstaging expectations by this highly symbolic and suggestive manner of entering Jerusalem.

Did the Romans regard Jesus' approach to Jerusalem with fear? Or ignore him as inconsequential? In *The Chosen*, the Roman leaders and their wives take various sides debating the impact of Jesus, from the sublime to the ridiculous to the radical. The most "radical" fear was that Jesus would precipitate another Maccabean insurrection, thus bringing a clamp-down by Tiberius (Emperor of Rome). Such fervor and fear are reflected in the gospels (see John 11:45-57).

Were high priest Caiaphas' words about "one man dying for the good of the nation" a spot-on prophecy? In *The Chosen*, yes, but John's Gospel presents Caiaphas' prophecy as ironic and unintentional (11:49-51). Caiaphas headed up **The Sanhedrin** which included 70 men who acted as a judicial body. It had its roots in Moses appointing 70 elders to administer over Israel and existed until 425 AD. The term "Sanhedrin" comes from the Greek word *sunedrion*, which means "sitting together." They met in the Temple every day except festivals and the Sabbath.

Was the excessive perfume Mary bought for Jesus meant for burial? Or a gift of love and devotion? Mary's over-the-top love for Jesus represents "a year's wages" (300 denarii), which Judas regards as "wasteful," but Jesus finds commendable, as it prepares him for a royal burial (Matthew 26:6-13; Mark 14:3-9; John 12:1-8).

Drive it Home Review and Respond: Worship, Pray, Share

"The main thing is to keep the main thing the main thing," said Stephen Covey. No doubt the prophet Micah would have agreed while stating just exactly what the main thing is:

> *He has told you, O man, what is good;*
>   *and what does the Lord require of you*
> *but to **do justice**, and to **love kindness**,*
>   *and to **walk humbly** with your God.*

Come Thou Fount –Shane and Shane
Type in URL: tinyurl.com/come-thou-fount-song (5:58 min.)

We Believe –Newsboys
Type in URL: tinyurl.com/we-believe (3:41 min.)

In Matthew 25:35-36. Jesus tells us where we can find him:

"I was hungry and you gave me food, I was thirsty and you gave me drink, I was a stranger and you welcomed me, [36] I was naked and you clothed me, I was sick and you visited me, I was in prison and you came to me."

12. *How would you sum up what God values from Micah 6?*

13. *Where might you look for Jesus according to Matthew 25?*

14. *How are you seeing Jesus' values impact your life?*

...In what ways do you want to see even more of an impact?

Video Insights Exodus 12 Summary *-2BeLikeChrist*
Type in URL: <u>tinyurl.com/Exodus-12-summary</u> 7:20 min.)
Thoughts:

_____

Does Matthew 25:31-46 teach that Salvation is by Works not by Faith? *-Theology on the Ground*
Type in URL: <u>tinyurl.com/Matthew-25-on-salvation</u> (9:32 min.)
Thoughts:

_____

What Does God Require of Me? *- Oneminutepreacher*
Type in URL: <u>tinyurl.com/What-does-God-require</u> (6:01 min.)
Thoughts:

_____

A. C. T. S. Prayer:

Adoration / Confession / Thanksgiving / Supplication / Steps

Examine where you are with the Lord and the priority of his kingdom. Take it to him in prayer:

ADORATION: *How can you praise God from whom all blessings flow?*

CONFESSION: *What do you need to confess and change?*

THANKSGIVING: *Which circumstances will you thankfully embrace?*

SUPPLICATION: *For whom and for what will you pray?*

Next STEPS: *What will you do with what you've learned? With whom?*

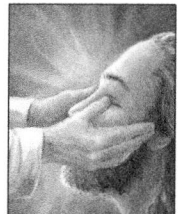

PRIOR **to** **STUDY**

"Your Faith Journey" on pages 160–168

NOTE FOR LEADERS: As mentioned, there is potential for an 11th Study if you'd like to add it (see page 132). Regardless of what you and your group decide to do, point out the *"Your Faith Journey"* section to be used, in one way or another, as a final overview and wrap-up for Season Four's guide.

Humble, Part 2 (Episode 8)

Study #10

FROM *The* **CHOSEN**

INTRO: It is good to weigh options, examine evidence, and compare theories. However, the time comes when a decision must be made. Will I go to college or start working? Take job A or job B? Get married or remain single? Live in place C or place D? Follow Jesus as Lord or reject his claims on my life? The time for that most weighty decision has arrived for the characters in *The Chosen*.

WATCH View Ep. 8A *(6 min., from 32:46 to 39:00)* > **Discuss**

INTRO: "Soon" has finally arrived. Jesus' purpose is about to be revealed. But first, his body must be prepared for burial.

DISCOVER *Read Aloud > Mark It Up > Discuss*

INTRO: Why would someone spend a year's wages on perfume for someone's feet? As you saw *in The Chosen*, this extravagant gift created even more controversy. As you study this passage, imagine the scene. **What do you see, hear, and smell?**

FROM The BIBLE

Mary Anoints Jesus at Bethany

John 12 Six days before the Passover, Jesus therefore came to Bethany, where Lazarus was, whom Jesus had raised from the dead. ² So they gave a dinner for him there. Martha served, and Lazarus was one of those reclining with him at table. ³ Mary therefore took a pound of expensive ointment made from pure nard, and anointed the feet of Jesus and wiped his feet with her hair. The house was filled with the fragrance of the perfume.

⁴ But Judas Iscariot, one of his disciples (he who was about to betray him), said, ⁵ "Why was this ointment not sold for three hundred denarii and given to the poor?" ⁶ He said this, not because he cared about the poor, but because he was a thief, and having charge of the moneybag he used to help himself to what was put into it.

⁷ Jesus said, "Leave her alone, so that she may keep it for the day of my burial. ⁸ For the poor you always have with you, but you do not always have me."

1. *Why do you think Mary did something this extravagant for Jesus?*

2. *Why was Judas offended by the gift?*

3. *What would have gone through your mind if you had been present?*

4. *Why did Jesus gladly accept the gift?*

WATCH **View Episode 8B** *(9 min., 39:00 to 47:43)* > **DISCUSS**

INTRO: After Mary's anointing of Jesus, the scene changes back to the secular world of the Romans. They, too, must decide about Jesus. The bottom-line is that keeping their job is their primary worry.

7. *What theories do the following characters express concerning Jesus?*

Pilate?

Herod?

Joanna?

Claudia?

WATCH **View Ep. 8C** *(14 min., from 47:43 to 1:01:26)* > **Discuss**

INTRO: Excitement, anticipation, or dread. Joanna and Claudia were correct. Something serious is about to happen. Jesus asks two of his disciples to prepare his way. *The Triumphal Entry* is celebrated as Palm Sunday, the week before Easter. **Watch as some in Jerusalem prepare for the original event.**

DISCOVER *Read Aloud > Mark It Up > Discuss*

INTRO: Jesus directs two of his disciples to find a colt (rather than a horse) to fulfill the prophecy of Zechariah 9:9 for his entry as the humble King.

FROM The BIBLE

Identify the directions Jesus gives to his disciples.

Jesus Entry to Jerusalem
MARK 11 Now when they drew near to Jerusalem, to Bethphage and Bethany, at the Mount of Olives, Jesus sent two of his disciples ² and said to them, "Go into the village in front of you, and immediately as you enter it you will find a colt tied, on which no one has ever sat. Untie it and bring it. ³ If anyone says to you, 'Why are you doing this?' say, 'The Lord has need of it and will send it back here immediately.'"

⁴ And they went away and found a colt tied at a door outside in the street, and they untied it. ⁵ And some of those standing there said to them, "What are you doing, untying the colt?" ⁶ And they told them what Jesus had said, and they let them go. ⁷ And they brought the colt to Jesus and threw their cloaks on it, and he sat on it. . . .

8. Zechariah 9:9 says:
> Rejoice greatly, O daughter of Zion!
>   Shout aloud, O daughter of Jerusalem!
> Behold, your king is coming to you;
>   righteous and having salvation is he,
> humble and mounted on a donkey,
>   on a colt, the foal of a donkey.

How do Jesus' instructions and actions mirror this prophecy?

WATCH **View Ep. 8D** *(5 min., from 1:01:26 to 1:06:30)* > **Discuss**

INTRO: There are many questions, few answers. What questions would you expect you'd have as Jesus starts his journey into Jerusalem?

FROM *The* **CHOSEN**

Look for reasons for following or rejecting Jesus.

The Words of Eternal Life

JOHN 6 [63] The words that I have spoken to you are spirit and life. [64] But there are some of you who do not believe." (For Jesus knew from the beginning who those were who did not believe, and who it was who would betray him.) [65] And he said, "This is why I told you that no one can come to me unless it is granted him by the Father."

[66] After this many of his disciples turned back and no longer walked with him. [67] So Jesus said to the twelve, "Do you want to go away as well?" [68] Simon Peter answered him, "Lord, to whom shall we go? You have the words of eternal life, [69] and we have believed, and have come to know, that you are the Holy One of God."

9. Jesus rides into the capital city of Israel as its kingly Messiah but in a different way than expected. *What does Jesus offer his followers?*

...What does he say is the requirement for following?

10. *Why does Peter decide to follow?*

11. *Where are you at right now in your relationship to Jesus?*

T-Shirt Design After watching > discovering > relating, What slogan would you write or draw on your T-Shirt?

Wrap up by sharing with your group.

Draft concepts or quotations for summarizing this study:

Final design:

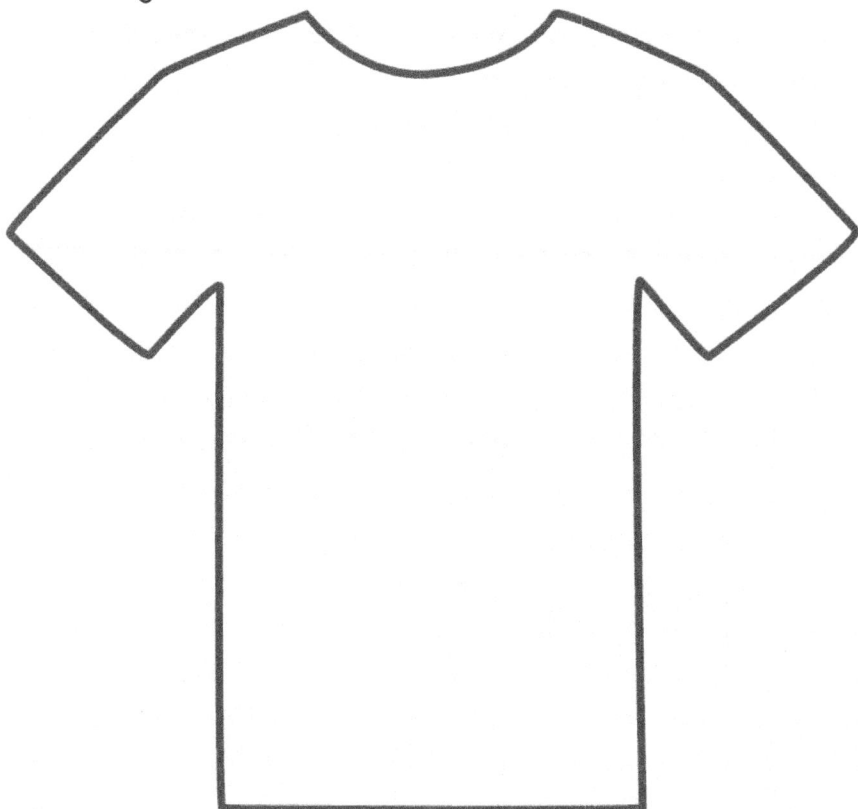

NOTES on Study #10 *Commentary and Historical Context*

John 12:1-8 – Mary Anoints Jesus at Bethany

- Pure nard was fit only for kings. Mary, well portrayed in *The Chosen*, got it. King Jesus puts all other kings to shame. Mary's act showed her appreciation that Jesus would mercifully include her and her family in his grace and that somehow, in her present, limited understanding, mercy could only come from a life-giving sacrifice for which she was preparing him.

- Others, especially Judas, completely missed the appropriateness of the perfume's expense (John 12:4-6). Jesus understood the honor of this extravagant anointing as a way to prepare him for his death and burial to come, the very sacrifice that would give the "poor" and the "poor in spirit," hope for this life and the one beyond.

- This gift cost 300 denarii, or the average of "a year's wages" for a day laborer in Palestine, who typically earned a denarii per day.

Mark 11:1-7 – Jesus Entry to Jerusalem

- Understanding the Messianic significance of this Triumphal Entry comes from the prophecy in Zechariah 9:9 (on page 152) that Jesus fulfills here. Jesus opts for riding a donkey instead of a horse. The time for him to come as a conquering king has not arrived (as it will when he returns as second time, see Revelation 19:11-21). For now, he comes as a humble king prepared to serve his people in the mission God has given him to complete (Mark 10:45).

- A young animal "that has never been ridden" is especially suitable for this use given the (spotless Lamb) sacrifice that was soon to be made (Numbers 19:2; Deuteronomy 21:3; 1 Samuel 6:7).

John 6:63-69 – The Words of Eternal Life

- This passage comes much earlier in Jesus' ministry than *The Chosen* portrays here. But the call to commitment is universal. Coming to Christ for salvation is never a human achievement or reason for boasting, but only possible by the Spirit drawing us.

That many were offended was expected by Jesus. Peter acts as a spokesman for the Twelve, who would soon carry the message to those who even now "go away," that there is mercy in the Cross.

REALISTIC But REAL?

That's plausible but did it happen?

What part did Yussif and Shmuel play in the Gospels? None. But in *The Chosen*, these fictional types flesh out the debates within the Sanhedrin and conversations with Jesus and his disciples. Yussif and Shmuel serve as convenient stand-ins for the larger audience that Jesus addresses in his speeches recorded in the Gospels. A legalistic Shmuel also serves as one more advocate for Judas to do what he's set on doing.

Was the bridle prophetic, as with the donkey? Or just a movie prop? A prop. This bridle is a creative element of *The Chosen* (introduced in Season Three, Episode 3) meant to show King Jesus in continuity as a "Son of David" as he prepares to enter Jerusalem one last time (Matthew 21:1-9; Mark 11:1-10; Luke 19:29-38; John 12:13-14).

The Chosen would have us believe the same bridle was passed down through 28 generations, from David............................ to Jesus in care of Mary and Joseph (see Luke 1:6-17).

Did Judas Iscariot steal from the disciples' common purse? Yes, according to John's Gospel (12:4-6) and *The Chosen*. The film gives a backstory (in episode 6) to Judas as a thief. When Matthew notices that there should be more money, he asks, where is the "other purse"? Now (in Episode 8) Judas' entrepreneurial and pragmatic side fleshes out his character more sympathetically. However, the Gospels are silent about such details, and we are left wondering about motives: *"Why? What really led to his betrayal?"*

Drive it Home *Review and Respond: Worship, Pray, Share*

Life is filled with limited choices. Peter understands this, and when asked by Jesus about his intentions to stay or to join others who were giving up on Jesus, he sized up the evidence and expressed the options: ***"Lord, to whom shall we go? You have the words of eternal life."***

Thank You Jesus *–Charity Gayle*
Type in URL: tinyurl.com/thank-you-Jesus (5:26 min.)

Breathe and We Fall Down *–Brooke Ligertwood and David Funk*
Type in URL: tinyurl.com/breathe-and-we-fall-down (11:09 min.)

Meditate on Peter's statement in John 6:68-69 above.

12. *To what extent have you thought through these two options?*

... At this time have you ever made the same wholehearted commitment as expressed in Peter's words?

... Why or why not?

Video Insights *Jesus Anointed at Bethany* –Joshua Hawkins
Type in URL: tinyurl.com/Jesus-anointed (11:25 min.)
Thoughts:

The Right Messiah –David Guzik
Type in URL: tinyurl.com/zechariah-9-9 (5:58 min.)
Thoughts:

The Sifting –Colin Smith
Type in URL: tinyurl.com/the-sifting (38:36 min.)
Thoughts:

A. C. T. S. Prayer:
Adoration / Confession / Thanksgiving / Supplication / Steps

Examine where you are with the Lord and the priority of his kingdom. Take it to him in prayer:

ADORATION: How can you praise God from whom all blessings flow?

CONFESSION: What do you need to confess and change?

THANKSGIVING: Which circumstances will you thankfully embrace?

SUPPLICATION: For whom and for what will you pray?

Next STEPS: What will you do with what you've learned? With whom?

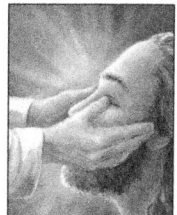

What follows provides
a look back to Season Four's studies and a look
forward to your life-experience. Use these questions
to extend your A-C-T-S reflection time, or you can
schedule another time to complete it.

Can you do so now? If not now, when?

Your Faith Journey Extend Your Drive it Home Session

15. First, read through pages 169-175 which describe the Gospels' characters and authors—their identity and calling. Also, for added input, look up the following link: jesusstudy.org/his-disciples

What has encouraged, challenged or surprised you about their stories?

Next, describe your "big picture" takeaway from the study BELOW, then on pages 162-163, and on the T-Shirt. Complete your study with a Wrap-Up on pages 165-167.

What are your takeaways from each study?

Study #1, Promises, *Episode 1 (pp. 17–29):*
> Luke 1:5–16, 39–45; Mark 6:14–29

Study #2, Confessions, Part 1, *Episode 2A and 2B (pp. 31–49):*
> Matthew 10:34–39; Matthew 16:13–20

Study #3, Confessions, Part 2, *Episode 2C (pp. 51–61):*
> John 9:1–6, 13–34; Matthew 23:1–17, 23–31

Study #4, Moon to Blood, *Episode 3 (pp. 63–75):*
> John 9:1–6, 13–34; Matthew 23:1–17, 23–31

Study #5, Calm Before, *Episode 4 (pp. 77–87):*
> Matthew 8:5–13; Mark 10:38–42

More takeaways?

Study #6, Sitting, Serving, Scheming, Episode 5 (pp. 89–101) Mark 7:1–12; Luke 10::21

The **FOURTH SEASON**

Study #7, Dedication, Episode 6, (pp. 103–117):
John 10:1–20; 10:22–39

Study #8, The Last Sign, Episode 7 (pp 119–131):
Luke 14:12–24; Luke 16:1–9

Study #9, Humble, Episode 8A, 8B and 8C (pp. 133–147):
Ex. 12:1–14; John 11:45–57: Matt. 25:31–45; Micah 6:6–8

Study #10, Humble, Part 2, Episode 8A, 8B, and 8C (pp 149–163):
John 12:1–8; Mark 11:1–7; John 6:63–68

T-Shirt Design As you look back over the entire season, What slogan would you write or draw on your T-Shirt?

Wrap up by sharing with others.

Draft concepts or quotations for the OVERALL SEASON:

Final design:

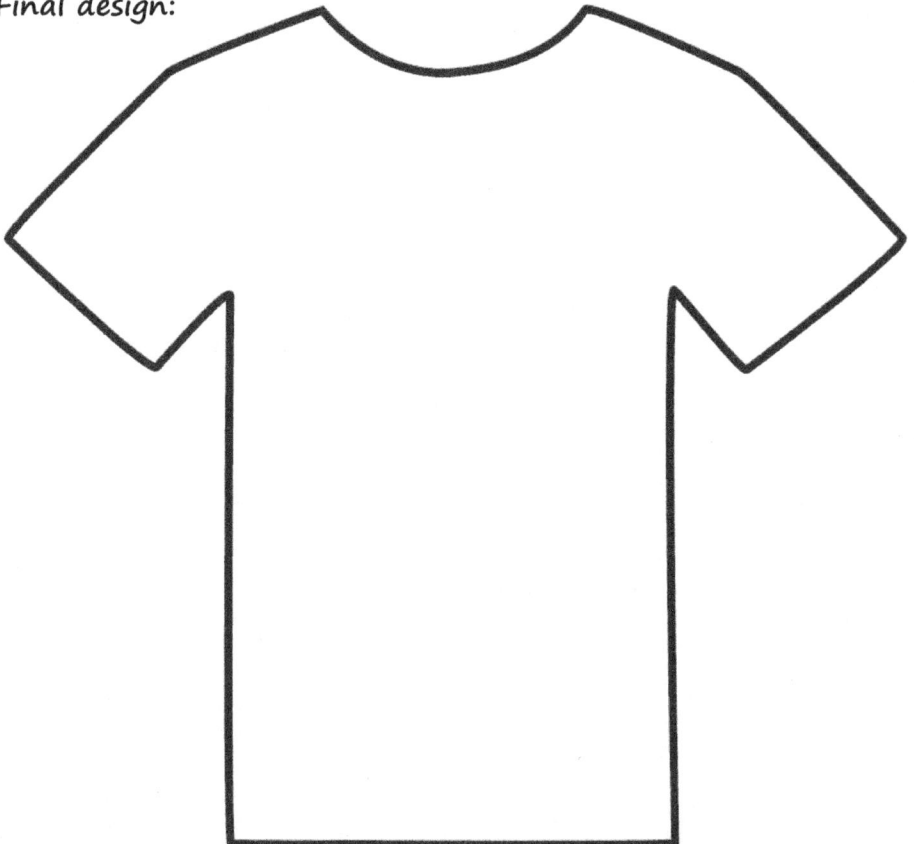

Final Wrap-Up   Getting to know Jesus

The Chosen does a good job depicting the "three steps forward, two steps back" process of following Jesus. Just look at the disciples. There's being intellectually convinced, and then there is knowing our need for a Savior leading to a willingness to repent and embrace what Jesus has done for us by faith. These are deep spiritual issues!

Can you recognize and even check what label fits you right now? If so, maybe that's a good place to start with the question: *Where am I at?*

___ skeptic....

Not convinced of the historical accuracy of the Bible, including the existence or importance of Jesus. Challenging miraculous events. Questioning how God could allow evil, how Christianity could be the "only way," or what about science? Wondering if *faith* is reasonable.

___ observer....

Maybe have gotten to know a Christian friend, been invited to attend worship, tried out a study group or a church project: Intrigued by Jesus and spiritual things, drawn to Bible stories about God's love, but un-sure about personal sin, the need for a Savior or how it relates to you.

___ seeker....

Searching for something more: hope, a sense of meaning or purpose, maybe a community of supportive friends. Questioning if there is more to life than money and the daily grind. Frustrated with self and the lack of consistency in character. Wondering if Jesus has some answers.

___ learner....

Openness to examine your beliefs with Jesus' teaching about himself and his purpose. Working to understand who God is as recorded in the Bible, and to engage with those pursuing the Christian faith. Looking to experience God's grace and to extend love and forgiveness.

___ follower...

Repent and embrace faith—forsaking our independence from God and pursuing Jesus as God. Looking to his sacrificial death as God's gift of grace and forgiveness in adopting us as his sons and daughters. Entering a lifelong commitment to him as your GREATEST TREASURE.

Final questions for contemplation (and sharing with others)

Do you increasingly find yourself caught up in Jesus' story?

Do you trust testimony regarding Jesus from Matthew, Mark, Luke and John to the extent that you are ready to take further steps to trust him?

Conversely, at the end of this study, do you need more evidence for some aspect of Jesus' life and teaching? What would be most helpful?

Wherever you are spiritually, allow us to recommend something that will likely help you grow toward Christ or grow in him, and here it is:

If Jesus says to love your enemies, try it out.

If he says to show hospitality like the Good Samaritan, do so.

If he wants you to help find lost sheep like a Good Shepherd, go for it.

As you "try on Jesus' teaching," you will find it not only making sense, but that you will also need to look to him for the wisdom, courage, and strength to take the risk of making some hard choices. Thankfully, in this journey of faith, his forgiveness is always close at hand.

Which teaching of Jesus would God have you "try on" right now?

In what ways do you need his help to do move ahead?

With whom can you share what you've learned and its impact on you?

A. C. T. S. Prayer:
Adoration / Confession / Thanksgiving / Supplication / Steps

Examine where you are with the Lord and the priority of his kingdom. Take it to him in prayer:

ADORATION: How can you praise God from whom all blessings flow?

CONFESSION: What do you need to confess and change?

THANKSGIVING: Which circumstances will you thankfully embrace?

SUPPLICATION: For whom and for what will you pray?

Next STEPS: What will you do with what you've learned? With whom?

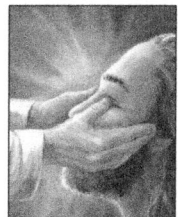

Your Faith Journey (for additional space, see page 202):

Background Notes The Four Gospels*

Early tradition identifies Matthew, Mark, Luke, and John as the ones who introduced Jesus to the First Century world and to ours. Their portrait of him is both historically unique and remarkably consistent.

MATTHEW: Given his occupation as a tax collector for the Roman government, we can only imagine the initial tension between Matthew (also called Levi) and the other disciples. But reconciliation lay at the heart of Jesus' message (see *The Sermon on the Mount,* Mathew 5-7). Matthew's Gospel emphasizes the interconnectedness between the Old and New Testaments and provides young believers a systematic tutorial on Jesus' teaching which is why it was put first in the NT.

MARK: This Gospel has been generally recognized as the account coming from Peter. Mark begins his first "sentence" with no verb: *The beginning of the Gospel about Jesus Christ, the Son of God*. His last sentence ends with the women fleeing Jesus' empty tomb *because they were afraid.* For Mark, Jesus is a man of action. To help believers facing persecution from the Roman state, Mark focuses on Jesus as the Suffering Servant who "came to serve" (Mark 10:45).

LUKE: An educated Greek physician and traveling companion of Paul, Luke authored the book of Acts and the Gospel that bears his name. Although Luke never met Jesus, he was acquainted with most of the key eyewitnesses who knew him (Luke 1:1-4). After extensive interviews with these contacts, Luke begins: *"Since I myself have carefully investigated everything from the beginning, it seemed good also to me to write an orderly account"* (Luke 1:3).

JOHN: A fisherman and brother of James, he writes, "In the beginning was the Word," offering a rather obvious parallel to the opening words of Genesis. In the "first Genesis," God spoke *Creation* into existence, and in the "second Genesis" God speaks *Redemption* into existence: "The Word became flesh and made his dwelling among us" (1:14). This "Word made flesh" is who John wants his readers to know.

The Gospels and John: Two Quick Overviews -Whiteboard Bible Study
tinyurl.com/four-gospels (10:40) / tinyurl.com/overview-john (8:01)

Mark is the shortest Gospel, likely written first (around AD 65) and orginating from the ministry of Peter. Many scholars believe Matthew and Luke had access to Mark because 76% of Mark's Gospel ends up in both Matthew and Luke and **97% of his Gospel ends up one or the other of them**. These three Synoptics (*similar summaries*) borrow from each other and additional independent sources as this chart suggests.

The content in **John's Gospel is 92% unique**. It covers a different time span than the others; it sets much of Jesus' ministry in Judaea; and it portrays him discoursing at length on theological matters (see the next page on John's uniqueness).

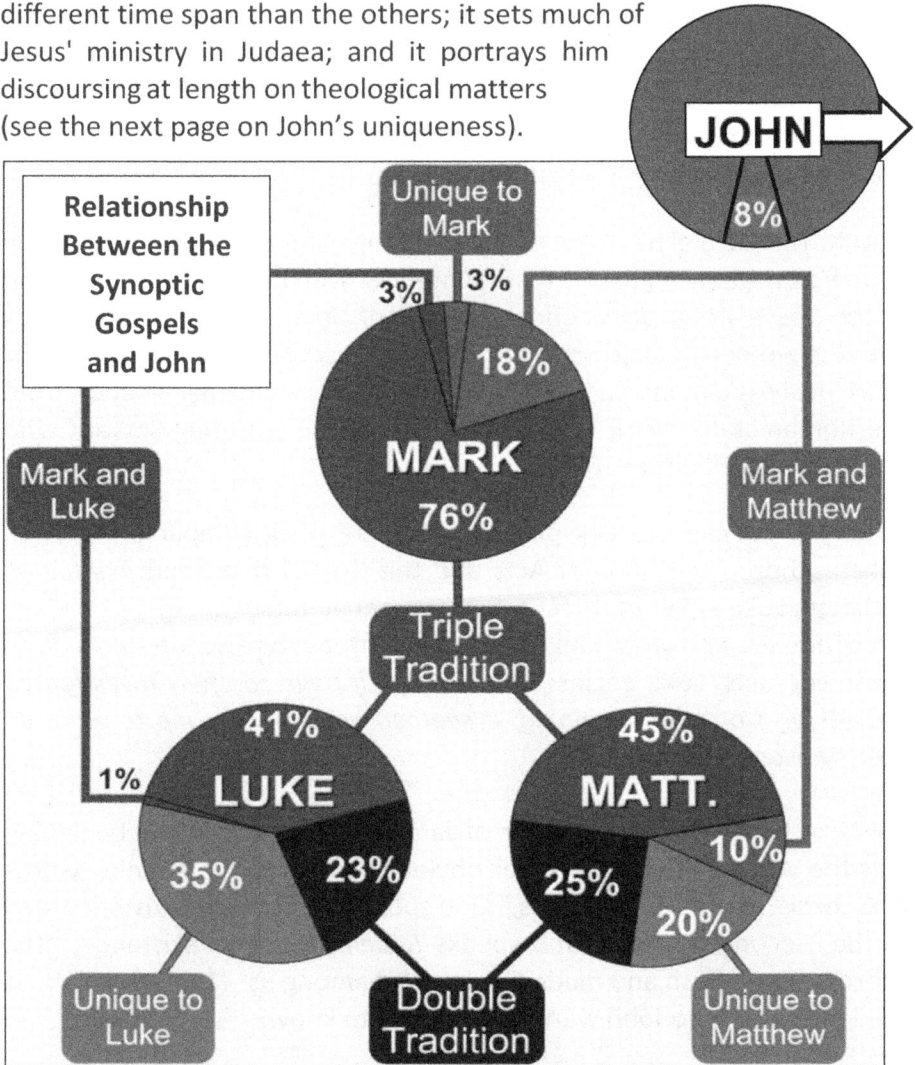

Relationship Between the Synoptic Gospels and John

JOHN 8%

Unique to Mark 3% | 3%
18%
MARK 76%

Mark and Luke

Mark and Matthew

Triple Tradition

41% **LUKE** 1%
35% 23%

45% **MATT.**
25% 10%
20%

Unique to Luke | Double Tradition | Unique to Matthew

The relationship between the Synoptic Gospels chart is courtesy wikimedia.org of: tinyurl.com/between-gospels Also see the web link on page 175 for more info.

John's Gospel provides seven signs

Of the 37 miracles recorded in the NT, John goes in-depth into seven of them to validate Jesus' Messianic claim. And, if that isn't enough to assert deity, the I AM statements, God's name first given to Moses in Exodus (see circle below), make clear who he claims to be— God himself.

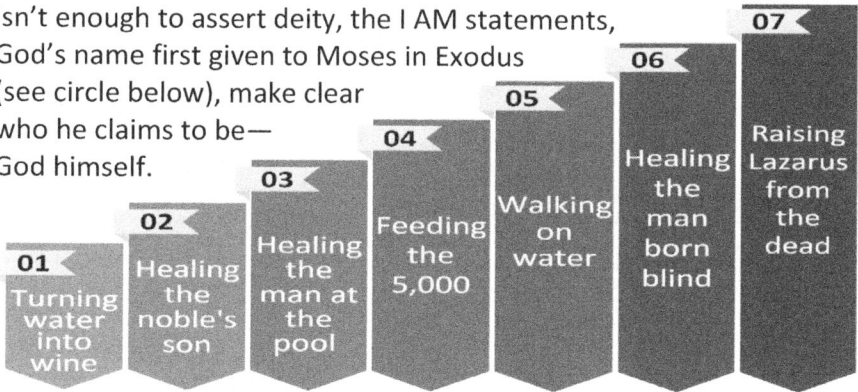

01
Turning water into wine

02
Healing the noble's son

03
Healing the man at the pool

04
Feeding the 5,000

05
Walking on water

06
Healing the man born blind

07
Raising Lazarus from the dead

John identifies Jesus' nature as "I AM"

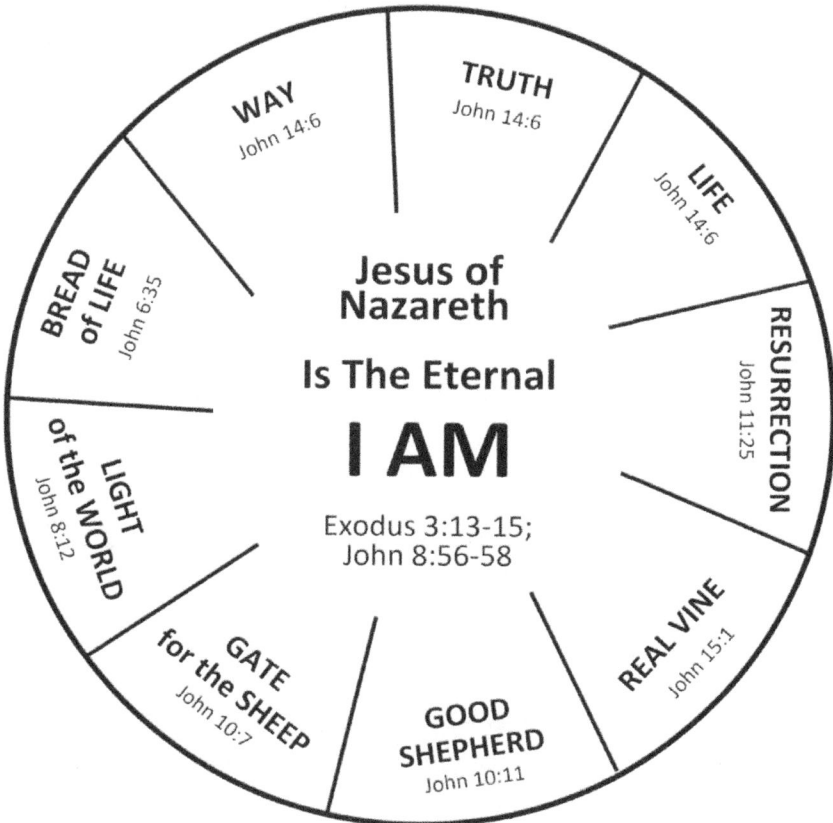

WAY
John 14:6

TRUTH
John 14:6

LIFE
John 14:6

BREAD of LIFE
John 6:35

Jesus of Nazareth

Is The Eternal

I AM

Exodus 3:13-15;
John 8:56-58

RESURRECTION
John 11:25

LIGHT of the WORLD
John 8:12

GATE for the SHEEP
John 10:7

GOOD SHEPHERD
John 10:11

REAL VINE
John 15:1

History's Most Audacious Story

Comparison of the Gospels				
	MARK	**MATTHEW**	**LUKE**	**JOHN**
Writer (Traditional)	Companion of Peter, the John Mark from Acts	Former tax collector (Levi) and one of the twelve	A Greek physician and traveling companion of Paul	Former fisherman, one of the twelve, beloved disciple
Date Written	**AD 63-70**	**AD 75-80**	**AD 80-85**	**AD 90-100**
Images of Christ	**Man of Action** Proclaims the kingdom of God and forgiveness of sin, Son of Man and Liberator, calling followers	**Master Teacher** Visited at birth by magi, new Moses and King to restore Israel as promised Messiah, Deliverer and Son of God	**Merciful Savior** Visited at birth by shepherds. The compassionate Champion. Loves the poor, children, women, outcasts	**The God-Man** The Logos, Word of God, Creator and Light of the World, Son of God, Lamb of God, Redeemer in total control
Written to:	**Romans**	**Jews**	**Greeks**	**Everyone**
The Author's Community	Christian community in Rome undergoing persecution	Jewish Christian community in Antioch, Syria	Theophilus (*Lover of God*) possibly represents all Christians (Greece)	Community of Jews, Gentiles, and Samaritans of Ephesus In Turkey
Theme: Jesus as	**Suffering Servant**	**Messiah King**	**Redeemer**	**Son of God**
General Theme	Jesus 'takes over" from John the Baptist as the Promised One, healing, forgiving. ("immediately")	Jesus teaches what it means to be a member of the Kingdom of Heaven and a growing disciple.	Jesus finds the lost and heals divisions among people. He shows compassion for those in need of help and hope.	Jesus is God, full of grace and truth. Salvation available for those who believe and commit their lives (7 signs).
Feature	**Miracles**	**Sermons**	**Parables**	**"I AM" Statements**
Historical Situation	The Romans subdue armed Jewish rebellions, Christians are experiencing persecution.	Written after Rome had destroyed Jerusalem whose destruction was prophesied by Jesus at the Temple.	Written when the persecution of Christians was intensifying throughout the Roman Empire.	Domitian mandated that all people worship him. Jewish leaders banned Christians from synagogues.
Caesars	Nero: AD 54-68	Vespasian and Titus: AD 70-81	Domitian: AD 81-96	Domitian: AD 81-96 Nerva: AD 96-98 Trajan: AD 98-117
Key Verses	10:45	16:13-20	19:10	20:30-31

Note: The disciples' images from *The Chosen* are used on the next page. The link and pages that follow have more information on each of them.

Jesus' disciples identity and calling: jesusstudy.org/his-disciples

Knowing those who knew him best

John the Baptist: Miraculously conceived shortly before his cousin Jesus, he proclaims Jesus, as foretold by Isaiah (40:3-5), calling Jews to repent in preparation for the Messiah. After a faithful ministry and baptizing Jesus, he is imprisoned and later beheaded for the threat he posed to Herod Antipas. Jesus identifies him as *the greatest of those born of women* (John 1:6-34; Matthew 3:1-17; 11:1-19; 14:1-12; Luke 1:5-25, 57-80).

Andrew: One of the first to follow Jesus, he brings his brother, Simon (Peter), right away. Together with fellow fishermen, James and John, Andrew leaves everything to follow Jesus after the miraculous catch. He also plays a key role in the feeding of the 5,000 (John 1:40-42; 6:8-9).

Simon Peter: This fisherman meets Jesus and is later renamed Peter, *the Rock*. He is brought to Jesus by his brother, Andrew, and follows Jesus then. He is well-known for walking (and sinking) on water, slicing off a soldier's ear, denying Jesus before his death, being a prominent leader in the early Christian movement, and for writing 1 and 2 Peter (Matthew 14:25-32; 16:13-28; Mark 14:66-72; John 1:40-42; Luke 5:1-11).

James and John: Along with Simon, they become Jesus' closest disciples. Appropriately nicknamed by Jesus as the "sons of thunder" (Luke 9:54), they were Simon's partners and, like him, they left everything to follow Jesus after the huge catch of fish (Mark 3:17; Luke 5:1-11). John goes on to write a Gospel, three letters, and the Book of Revelation.

Matthew: Also known as Levi, is a despised tax collector when Jesus calls him from his tax booth to follow Him. He *left everything and followed him,* and invites many friends and coworkers to a dinner with Jesus (Luke 5:27-32). He authors the Gospel of Matthew.

Mary Magdalene: One of several women mentioned in Luke 8:2-3 who had been "cured of evil spirits and diseases" and was following Jesus. Having been delivered from seven demons, she is with Jesus at the cross and is the first one to whom Jesus appears after the Crucifixion (Luke 8:2-3; John 19:25-27; John 20:1-18).

James the Less (*micros,* meaning "little" or "young") and **Thaddeus:** Two lesser-known disciples: "Little James," a son of Alphaeus (Mark 3:18), could have been Matthew's brother (also a son of Alphaeus, Mark 2:14), but is never identified as such. Thaddeus, aka Jude/Judas, may have gotten his nickname (meaning "breast child" or "mama's boy") to distinguish him from the other Judas, to avoid negative connotations.

Thomas (aka Didymus, or "twin"): Best known for doubting: *Unless I see the nail marks in his hands... I will not believe* (John 20:25). Thomas could, maybe more accurately, be called *logical.* Regardless, we see a whole-hearted passion, even an openness to die with Jesus (11:16), and fear of missing him (14:5). Thomas, the last of The Twelve to see Jesus after the resurrection, upon seeing him proclaims, *My Lord and my God* (20:24-29).

Mary, mother of Jesus: She is the teenager God chose to give birth to Jesus, who was conceived in her by the Holy Spirit. She raises Jesus with **Joseph,** who married her after an angel appears to him in a dream, and who probably died before Jesus began his adult ministry. She weeps at the Crucifixion, witnesses the resurrected Christ, and, along with at least some of her other children (Acts 1:14), is part of the early church (Luke 1:26-56; 2:5-7; 8:19-21; John 2:1-12; 19:25-27).

Philip is a disciple of John the Baptist, and a friend of Andrew. He changes allegiance from John to Jesus, and seeks out a friend, **Nathanael,** who wonders aloud, *Can anything good come out of Nazareth?* Philp seemingly quotes Jesus, *Come and see!* Nathanael does and is amazed that Jesus "saw him" before they meet: *Before Philip called you, when you were under the fig tree, I saw you.*

Simon (the Zealot) is distinct from Simon (Peter). We don't know a lot about him from the gospel record other than his association with the Zealots, a group of Jewish insurrectionists who opposed Roman rule. Without much to go on, there has been a wide variety of speculation. Some options are: the same person as Simeon of Jerusalem who became an early Christian leader, Simon, the brother of Jesus, perhaps a cousin of Jesus, or even a son of Joseph from a previous marriage.

Judas (Iscariot)—was a name probably given to him as a designation of his native place, Kerioth, a town in Judah. In *The Chosen* he is introduced as the last of the disciples to join, but the New Testament only indicates that he was one of the Twelve, not when he joined.

Spoiler Alert! What happens next...

Episode 1: At this printing the filming of *Season Five* is completed but not yet available. Hey, if you have access to the scripts, let us know!

Episode 2:

Episode 3:

Episode 4:

Episode 5:

Episode 6:

Episode 7:

Episode 8:

MARK where it happened on the map

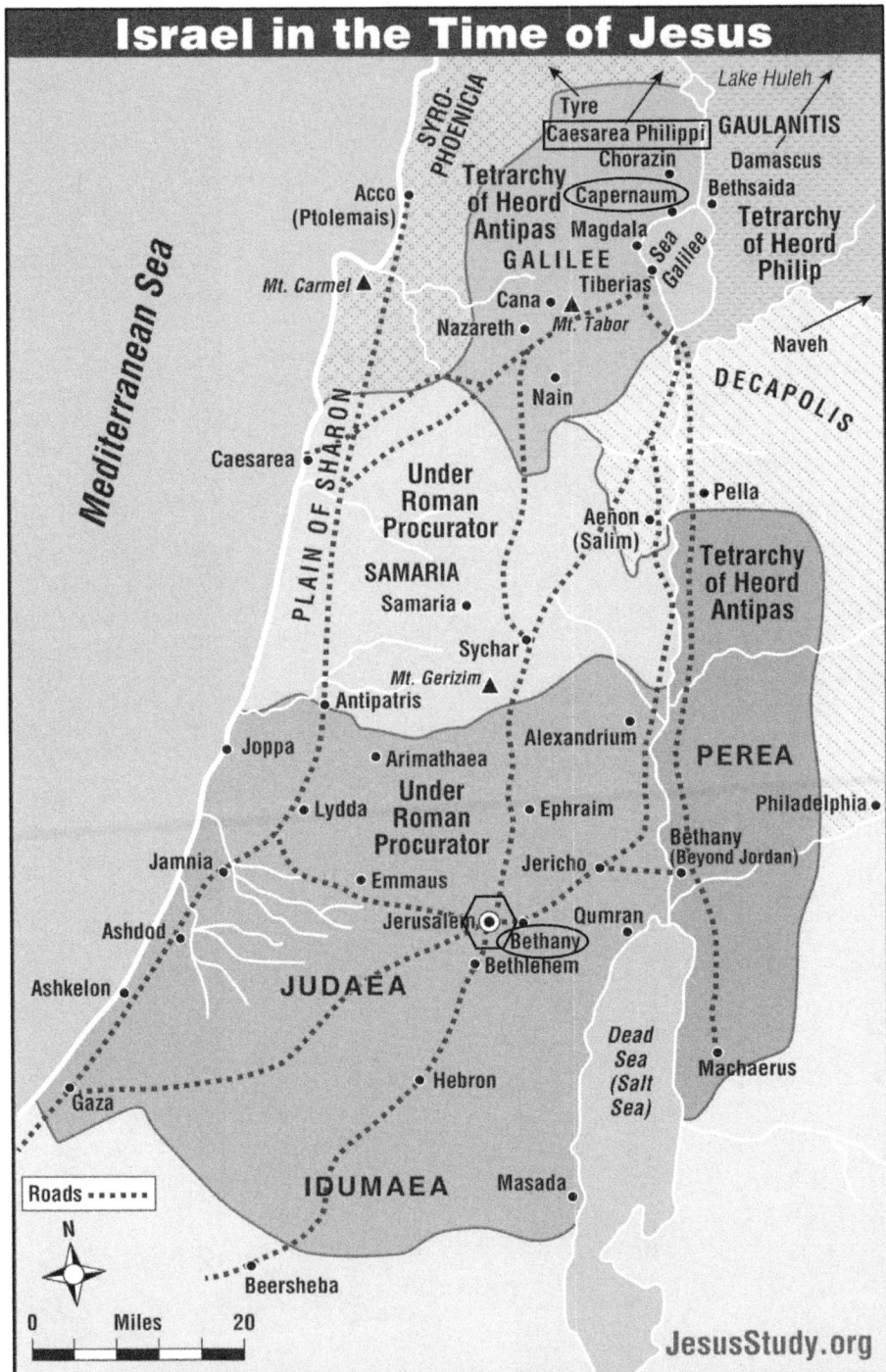

Israel in the Time of Jesus

RECORD locations cited and what happened there:

- Caesarea Philippi: Matthew 16:13, Peter's confession (p. 41)

- Capernaum: Matthew 8:5, Site of centurion's faith (p. 78)

- Jerusalem: Mark 10:32, Israel's capital (p. 80, 107)

- Bethany: John 11:1, Lazarus, Mary and Martha (p. 109)

-

-

-

-

-

-

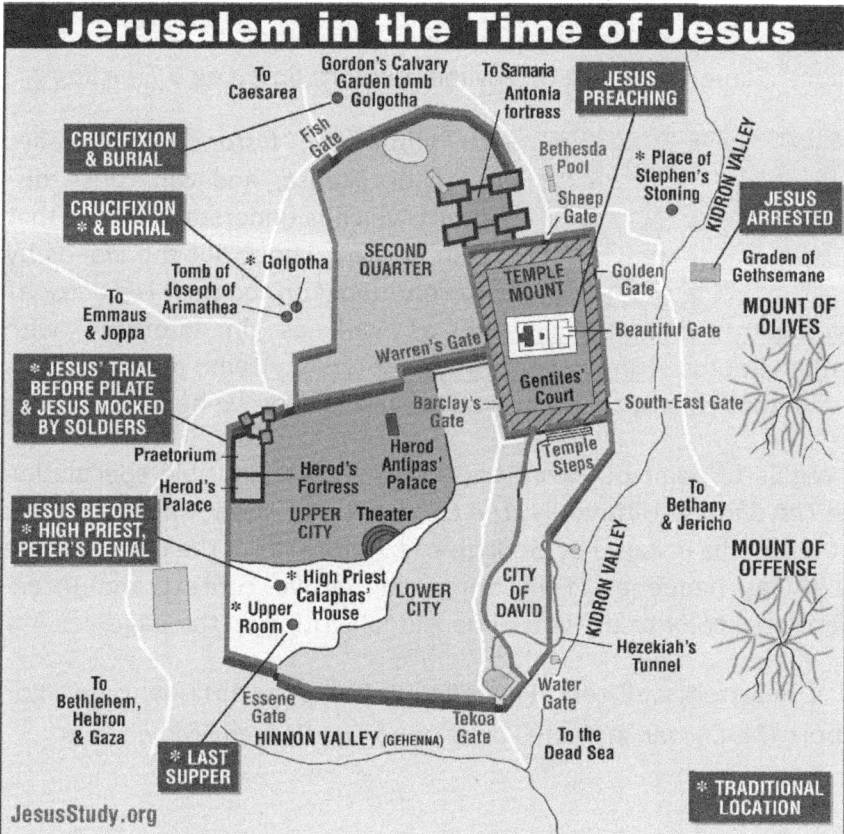

Jerusalem in the Time of Jesus

Can you trust The Chosen?

Some have raised questions about the authenticity of *The Chosen*—which is what this guide's *Realistic But Real?* sections highlight. An analogy to Bible translation could be made in this regard.

Some Bible translations strictly follow the original Hebrew and Greek, but such very literal renditions can make it difficult to read in other languages. Other translations focus on meaning by reworking sentence structures into a better, native-reading format: a "dynamic equivalent." (*The Chosen Study* uses one slightly tilted toward literal: ESV.)

Still other "translations" paraphrase the original words, or even add interpretation, thus amplifying (but not contradicting) the meaning.

Every film enactment of biblical events falls somewhere on a similar spectrum: from a literal (word-for-word) depiction, to a dynamic equivalent, to a non-literal paraphrase. In the case of *The Chosen*, it would be fair to characterize it as beyond paraphrase to an "amplified version." Some would use this byline under it: *Based on a True Story*.

Such "non-literal," *historical fiction* relies on artistic license, and can cause discomfort which is understandable. If that is true for you, check out the videos by Dallas entitled: *Can you trust The Chosen?* (tinyurl.com/trusting-the-chosen), as well as an interview with Jonathan Roumie, (tinyurl.com/roumie-interview), who portrays Jesus. These videos convey their perspective and may prove helpful.

We regularly point out what happened versus plausible speculation from *The Chosen*. Ultimately, *The Chosen* is a TV show, and the Bible is the only media inspired by God, given to inform us of the truth and the way things happened. Film brings supportive context and three-dimensional color to the two-dimensional writing on the page.

Dallas' heartfelt, well-conceived mission (see page 15) is why we vigorously support *The Chosen* and have developed *The Chosen Study*.

Leaders Notes

The Chosen Vision: Dallas and his team share the goal of *reaching a billion people with the message of Jesus*. Our "loaves and fish" effort joins their far-reaching aspirations by **helping study leaders facilitate discussions about Jesus with everyone we know, and to see people grow into and as Christ followers.**

If you're on the fence about leading, consider Jesus' challenge to Andrew in Episode 8 of Season One about traveling through the hated Samaritan territory, a place considered unclean and dangerous: *Did you join me for safety reasons?*

So, you're interested in leading a Chosen Study? Here's what to do:

Gather a Core Team

**The Chosen Study Team
is a small group with a big purpose.**
Draw together a core group made up of those who have seen "something different" in Jesus and want others to experience that difference. The team meets together regularly (shoot for weekly) to support the group process and pray. They plan, oversee the food, and invite friends and family to join in. This team can take on the following roles:

–***The Group Leader*** oversees the group's study and discussion process and seeks to foster one-on-one friendship evangelism and discipleship within the group. We encourage the Group Leader to model servant leadership within the group and to send out weekly emails.

–***The Prayer Team Promoter*** finds ways to support the Study in prayer.

–***The Meal Organizer*** oversees the food. See *Resources* at the website for theme potluck sign-up sheets. Meal Organizers can also keep in touch during the week with group emails. (The first meal will likely be something like a pizza instead of a planned potluck. See page 185.)

–*Child Care Helper* for younger families who need such help to come.

–*Set-Up/Sign-Up/Name Tag/Greeter* should be designated, especially for larger groups. For the people who may not feel comfortable at first, you'll want to extend hospitality and friendship from the start.

– *"Tech Person"* to oversee film management—stopping and starting.

–*Small Group Facilitators* (for larger studies, eight or more) oversee their group. **It is best to sit around small tables with just four to six others** (and helpful to separate spouses), rotating members weekly.

–*Day-Long or Weekend Event Organizer* (see page 16 and the website).

FYI: There are two series. **The Chosen Series** includes all **8 Episodes in 10 studies.** *The Bible Series* leaves out much of the back story and presents **20 scenes in 20 studies.** (See pages 193-195 and the website for these options.)

Be Inclusive of Everyone

Who to invite? Everyone who is open to come: The religious, the skeptics, the non-religious, the seekers—you name it. This is to be a fun, interactive place that values and respects everyone.

We hope group members share differences of opinion and viewpoints from all over the spiritual map. We're glad about that. Each person brings their own background. We're not here to judge. We love to stir up discussion and hear unaccustomed perspectives. As Jesus said to Simon in season one: *Get used to different!*

Sharing and Prayer: To respect where people are spiritually, encourage believers to **avoid insider-type sharing**—which can characterize typical Bible study groups. (Also, prayer should primarily take place before you come or after you leave, not during group time.) A Chosen Study is a **skeptic- and seeker-friendly outreach group** for mutual learning, and to develop deeper friendships both inside and outside the group context.

Get the Word Out

Direct Invitation: Yes, we still do that, right?! Indeed, it is by far the most effective means.

Email Invitation: Get the word out quickly by sending a link to the trailer, website, and a flyer attachment.

Text Invitation: Send out a photo, or better yet, a digital photo (JPG) of your flyer, and an active link to the trailer and website.

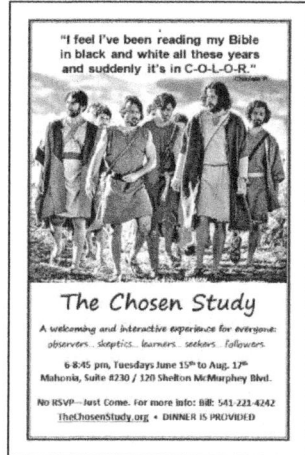

"I feel I've been reading my Bible in black and white all these years and suddenly it's in C-O-L-O-R."

The Chosen Study

A welcoming and interactive experience for everyone: observers . skeptics . learners . seekers . followers

6-8:45 pm, Tuesdays June 15th to Aug. 17th
Mahonia, Suite #230 / 120 Shelton McMurphey Blvd.

No RSVP—Just Come. For more info: Bill 541-221-4242
TheChosenStudy.org • DINNER IS PROVIDED

Flyers: Contact us at our website to receive sample flyers in MS Word that you can adapt and print or make up your own to hand out.

Create a Facebook Event and **Church Announcements** to the masses.

Plan for Food

Our studies seek to connect us to God AND to each other. What better way to bring people together than by sharing food and conversation? We encourage starting with a meal, potluck or, at least, finger food. The role of overseeing the meals is a tremendous service to the group.

Lead and Facilitate the Group

You can begin small—with just one friend, one-on-one, or gather a group. Pray, invite, read, and underline the key points on pages 8-15 and 183-190. The leader's notes integrated along the way are for both current and future leaders to gain confidence in how to facilitate their groups.

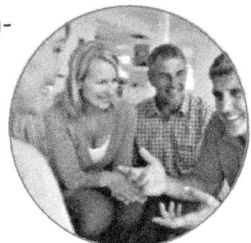

Multiply Your Efforts—*through small/large (8+) group combos*

Combining small groups within a larger group:
When a group starts large or grows larger—*to eight or more*—the larger size presents unique opportunities. Small groups provide a *depth* of intimacy which allows members to participate more. Larger group interaction can then draw out the very best insights from the small group discussions to offer a greater *breadth* of give-and-take sharing.

Day-Long or Weekend Event Organizer (see page 16 and the website).

This combination **provides for two (shorter) discussion times**, with the best of both dynamics, and gives group leaders the role of a "dialogical" (two-way), not "monological" (one-way), teacher. After each small group time, the leader brings together the larger group for a "check-in" to highlight what was discussed within the small groups.

A small/large group combination **offers a chance for the core team to facilitate the smaller groups**. The goal is to foster a guided conversation. This, likewise, is true for a large group leader on a larger scale. Quality, dialogical teaching brings a soft touch to the group sharing by focusing on the best insights gleaned from the small groups.

Larger groups thus **provide discipleship opportunities** for group members to step into the role of small group facilitators, as part of the core Chosen Study team. The goal is to help equip an increasing number of these leaders to multiply their outreach efforts in the lives of others. The challenge during the group time is to keep up the pace.

If you're currently a group member with such aspirations, feel free to study through the guide notes, go through the website and look for an opportunity to join a team, or to start your own Chosen Study!

For Leader Support: jesusstudy.org/contact

The website's primary purpose is to equip current and future leaders to make disciples and provide a community of discipleship for those using *The Chosen* for outreach and growth. *How can we serve you?*

Eight Group Ground Rules to Enhance Your Experience

1. **The Leader** is a **facilitator** of discussion, guiding the group through questions rather than statements. He or she is responsible to **prepare for and oversee group interaction** and to **help with outreach**.

2. **The Guide** makes for a valuable personal study but is especially set up to help **current and future leaders** facilitate watching, study, and discussion in one-to-one, and in small/large group settings.

3. **Prior Preparation** is not expected. We do, however, have a **Drive it Home** reflection time and **Video Insights** for post-Study follow-up.

4. **Each Group Member** "owns the group," and is thus seen as a key contributor of comments and questions. **Talkative members** should defer to others and **quiet members**, speak out. *The conversation engagement around the circle should look like a pinball machine!*

5. **Group Focus** is controlled by its purpose. *The Chosen* Study allows the episode and Scripture passage to **govern the discussion**, rather than Bible commentaries or cross referencing. Tangents are to be avoided or at least "tabled," until after the group meeting is over.

6. **Personal Growth** from studying Jesus is our goal. Such growth naturally includes a **focus on humility** and **child-like faith**.

7. **Group Growth** happens as **friendships form and deepen**. Members should see themselves as more than just a study group, but as a community where consistency, accountability, self-disclosure, empathy, and reaching out to others are key characteristics.

8. **Avoid making "guest appearances."** Don't let *stay-at-home feelings* or distractions dictate whether you come. **Commit to attend** every meeting. Take this gathering seriously—for you and for others.

Fight "those feelings" and the distractions by <u>signing this challenge</u>:

Unless out-of-town or near death's door, I'll be there: _____

Yes, bear down and GO FOR IT! Your name here.

Eight Don'ts of Leading Group Discussions

You're NOT a teacher, you're *a facilitator*. To lead a highly productive group discussion, start with what NOT to do and you're halfway there!

1. **Don't answer your own questions.** Otherwise, the group will look to you as "the teacher" rather than "the facilitator." You're not just the questioner. You should participate like any member, but don't be the first one to answer your own question.

2. **Don't over-talk.** Groups with an overtalkative leader will often sit back—in boredom! 90% of what we hear we forget, but 90% of what we say, we remember. So, your goal is to get your group talking. Get them remembering. Get them learning.

3. **Don't be afraid of silence.** Silence may mean you need to rephrase the question, but if you "bail out your group" when silent, you set a bad precedent. To exercise patience, count in your head from 100 to 0 before answering—then, only if you must. Oh, yes, they'll talk!

4. **Don't be content with just one answer.** For every written question feel free to ask a follow-up question or two, like: "Does anyone else have a thought?" This allows several people to respond.

5. **Don't expect group members to respond with an answer each time.** They'll be tempted to look straight at you solely, especially when the group is new. Instead, you want them talking to each other, so you don't have to be the "discussion hub" (see page 190).

6. **Don't reject an answer as wrong.** Respond to questionable answers by asking, "How did you come to that conclusion?" or "There's probably a difference of opinion here. Does anyone else have another way of looking at this?" Be affirming to everyone.

7. **Don't be afraid of controversy.** Different opinions are a good thing.

8. **Don't allow the group to end late.** If the discussion proves fruitful, end on time. Don't let the group drag on, but for those who choose to stay, give opportunity to discuss the issue in more depth.

Eight Do's of Leading Group Discussions

You don't need to be an expert or trained teacher to lead a discussion group. Your role is that of a **facilitator**, one who guides others into a productive conversation centering on key points of the film clips and Bible studies. It's an honor to be able to serve your group in this way.

1. **Bring along your own curiosity and have fun with it.** Good start!

2. **Pace the study.** It's the leader's responsibility to both start and end on time. Keep up a flexible pace with one eye on the clock and the other on the content. There may be more questions than you have time for, so, if necessary, skip some questions. Press ahead!

3. **Give members the chance to study on their own.** They are free to do so—or not. There is no expectation of prior preparation.

4. **Have the Scripture read aloud.** Ask a group member to read. Some feel uncomfortable doing so in public, so don't make a surprise assignment unless you know they are willing and are good at it.

5. **Be on the alert for overtalkative people.** Someone who over-talks can squeeze the life out of a group. If this is a problem, engage with that group member after the meeting, and enlist their help to join you in your goal to get everyone involved in the discussion.

6. **Involve everyone, more or less equally.** Sit across from quiet people to draw them out, and next to talkative people to make less eye contact. If helpful, go around the circle with a question.

7. **Keep the discussion on track by avoiding tangents**. Tangents may seem important but can hurt purposeful discussion, leading the group to talk about less important things. "Important tangents" provide opportunities for conversation outside the group's time.

8. **Conduct a discussion first with general, then specific questions.** Your goal in NOT to get into one-and-done responses; rather, your goal is to start an engaging dialogue with several people responding to a particular question in a back-and-forth way (see next page).

Facilitating Group Interaction: Monological vs. Dialogical

If tables (small round or rectangle) are available, they are preferred for the meals and for group study (of ideally four to six participants each).

Dialogical interaction engages wide-ranging participation. Such give-and-take discussion sparked by the *table leader* and the *upfront leader* is desired. **Interaction from a leader's question is visualized below:**

Inferior Monological Interaction   Superior Dialogical Interaction

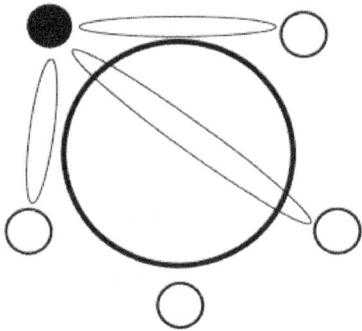

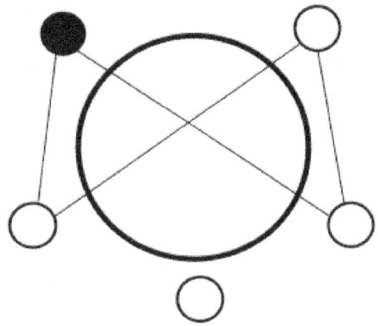

Small/Larger Group Combination—Can Work with Eight or More

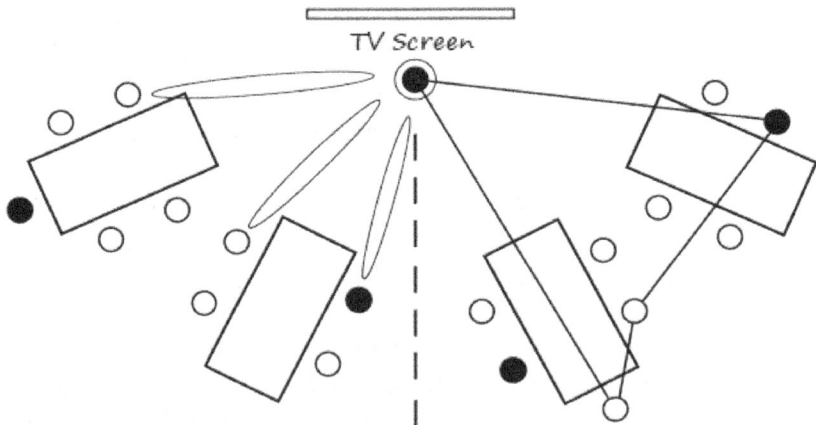

TV Screen

Dialogical leading *facilitates interaction* among your group members and prevents you from "brokering" the participants' comments with your own or monopolizing the discussion as seen above. As a leader you can participate, but your goal is to get others talking. **Remember: 90% of what you say they'll forget, but 90% of what you get them to say, they'll remember! So, get them get them talking and learning!!**

The JESUS STUDY

Have you seen something different in Jesus?

Join a Jesus Study Team and consider becoming a

Jesus Study Leader

Leader's Notes: What applies most to you and your group?

-

-

-

-

-

-

Your Chosen Group: Names, info., prayer concerns, etc.

-

-

-

-

-

-

-

-

Your Chosen Group: Names, info., prayer concerns, etc.

-
-
-
-
-
-
-
-
-
-
-
-
-
-
-
-

Note: For a sign-up sheet to print, see JesusStudy.org under *Resources*.

Study Resources

The JESUS STUDY

We do have a variety of guides available on Amazon or other retailers. Check the website for volume discounts: jesusstudy.org/order-guides

The Chosen Study Library

For: skeptics... observers... seekers... learners... followers.

THE CHOSEN STUDY
10 Studies from 8 Episodes in Each Guide

Season 1	Season 2	Season 3	Season 4	Season 5	Season 6	Season 7

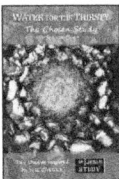    

WATER   HOPE   FOOD   SIGHT

THE BIBLE IN THE CHOSEN
20 Studies from 20 Scenes in Each Guide

Season 1	Season 2	Season 3	Season 4	Season 5	Season 6	Season 7

    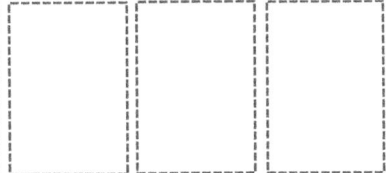

Find the (eventual) 140 YouTube Chosen Scene Playlist at:
tinyurl.com/chosen-playlist-1 (others: -2, -3, -4, -5, -6, -7)

THE CHOSEN SERIES (8 Episodes in 10 Studies each)

SEVEN Chosen Studies (watching full episodes blended with texts)

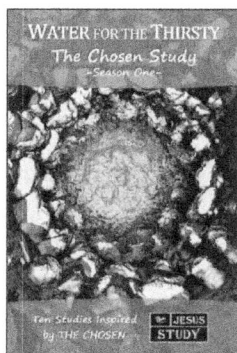

***The Chosen Study:* Season One,** focuses on Simon, Matthew, Andrew, Nicodemus, and Mary Magdalene as they encounter Jesus. This guide, based on the *The Chosen*, covers all the backstory and will give you and your group an in-depth appreciation of his followers' unexpected changes of fortune in getting to know him.

***The Chosen Study:* Season Two,** guides you and your group into Act Two of Jesus' life and ministry with his followers unsure of where this is all going.

Here we meet the remaining disciples, such as Nathanael, who is despondent over a career in shambles, only to be given a new vocation by Jesus. Besides him, there are a host of others with physical, mental, and emotional infirmities and demon-possession that, up to now, have been impossible to overcome.

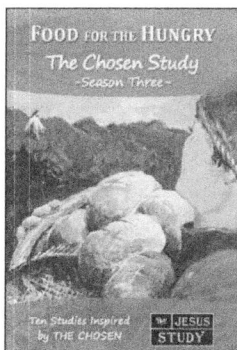

***The Chosen Study:* Season Three,** picks up with the famous *Sermon on the Mount* which sets the stage for the disciples taking a deep look into their own spiritual lives. The Study concludes with the *Feeding of the 5000* and with Jesus and Simon walking on the water.

***The Chosen Study:* Season Four** continues with Jesus and the disciples finding increasing opposition to Jesus' messianic claims especially from the Jewish religious leaders.

***The Chosen Study:* Seasons Five, Six and Seven** completes the most audacious story ever told. We look forward to watching the *The Chosen's* version.

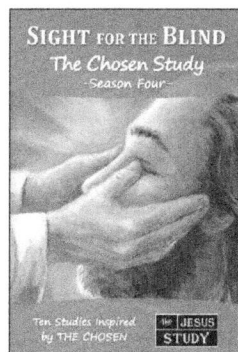

THE BIBLE SERIES (20 Studies from 20 Scenes)

SEVEN The Bible in The Chosen (less backstory, scenes with passages)

–SEASON ONE Study Guide   **–SEASON TWO Study Guide**

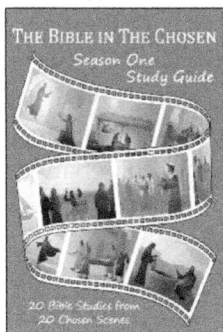

These guides take individuals or groups through Bible passages directly referenced throughout *The Chosen*. In so doing, much of the backstory is left out and a scene playlist is used instead. See the Youtube playlists at: tinyurl.com/chosen-playlist

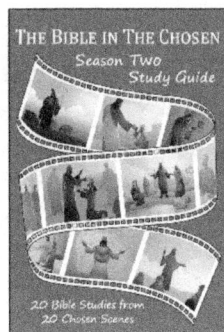

–SEASONS THREE, FOUR, FIVE, SIX and SEVEN

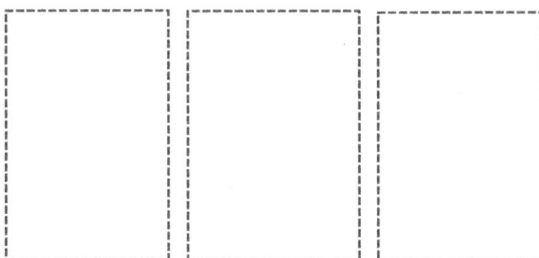

One-Time Chosen Christmas Event

Christmas with The Chosen: Holy Night This episode can be used as a *come-one-come-all event* (content starts at 31:00) before Christmas. Watching and discussing this episode could also act as a winter-quarter (January) kickoff for a new group: tinyurl.com/chosen-christmas

Going Inward: The Chosen Devotionals

The Chosen: 40 Days with Jesus provides a new devotional for each season to extend your experience throughout the week. You divide the 40 devotional readings into five per week: thechosengifts.com

THE BIBLE SERIES for other "Jesus Films"

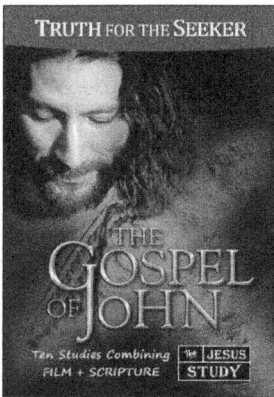

We're spoiled by *The Chosen*, but there are other quality, biblical movies, and *Jesus films* out there which we have adapted in a similar way to *The Chosen Study*:

The John Study is a ten-week series based on the 2003 movie entitled *The Life of Jesus*. This three-hour film is a word-for-word portrayal of John's Gospel from the *Good News Bible* translation: tinyurl.com/the-john-study-guide

The Risen Study is likewise a ten-week series based on a 2016 film entitled *RISEN*. This study follows the movie which begins with Jesus' death on the cross. A religious leader is granted permission to have him buried in his family's tomb and Pontius Pilate posts guards to ensure rumors of "a resurrection" don't take hold in Jerusalem.

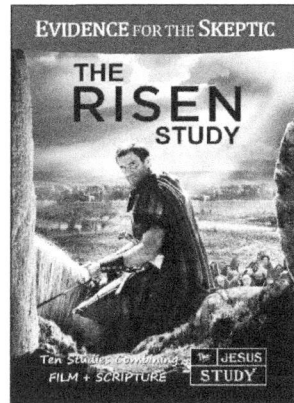

When the tomb ends up empty, Pilate's tribune, Clavius, is tasked with finding the body. In the process Clavius finds much more.

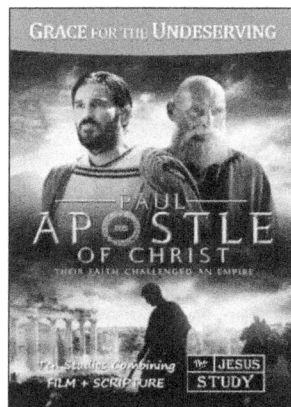

The Paul Study is a ten-week series based on a 2018 film entitled *Paul: Apostle of Christ*. Our study follows the movie with Paul in a Roman prison near the end of his life. Other local believers struggle with intensely hostile authorities toward them as well.

Luke, Paul's former traveling companion, is desperate to find Paul and to help him get a written record of the gospel out to the world he will soon leave behind.

The John, Risen and Paul studies make for a superb three-part series.

Bible apps, online access

Excellent for reading: YouVersion.com
Excellent for studying: BilbeGateway.com
Excellent for learning: BibleProject.com

Going Deeper: Journaling NT

Apply the *Mark-It-Up* study method to the entire New Testament with this double-spaced format for study and note-taking. To find out more about this NT: tinyurl.com/journal-nt

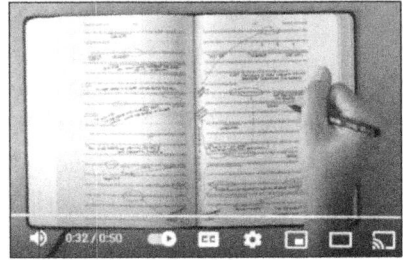

THE COUPLE SERIES

Are you getting all the romance, passion and joy you want in your relationship? Wouldn't you like to.....

- *Tell your partner how he or she can fully love you?*
- *Be fully listened to and completely understood in the process?*
- *Be nurtured and cherished in the unique way you feel loved?*

When it comes to the opposite sex, the intimacy rules are different!
This book will help you understand and overcome those differences by sharing an ordinary couple's extraordinary weekend of intimate conversations.

Sarah and Matt get away from the house, the kids and their daily lives to listen to each other's hearts, explore their differences and deepen their connection. Intimate Conversations enhances the lessons of their free-wheeling dialogue with practical how-to sections inviting readers to explore their own hearts and those of their partners: tinyurl.com/for-couples

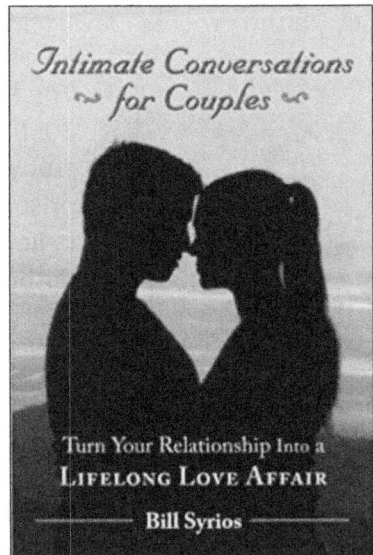

Intimate Conversations for Couples

Turn Your Relationship Into a
LIFELONG LOVE AFFAIR

Bill Syrios

Leadership Resources

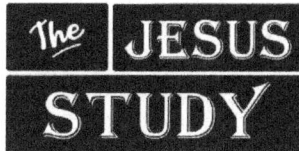

The JESUS STUDY

Our desire is to help church pastoral staff equip leaders to facilitate vibrant, "evangelizing, discipleship" communities that draw people in to watch, discover and relate to Jesus. When it comes to these studies, we've been there, done that. So, let us know how we can serve you.

Why make the change from
Bible Study 1.0 to Bible Study 2.0 ?

"Bible Study 1.0"—with its cognitive, all-talk, text-heavy or once-over-lightly approach—is what many of us grew up with and loved.

But this approach is not communicating well to our visual generation who instead seek visible learning via YouTube, video games, zoom, and webinar broadcasts on our devices. This visual experience has completely taken over our lives, shrunk our attention spans, and, yes, become the basis of most learning for every generation.

Into this milieu, enter "Bible Study 2.0," aka, *The Jesus Study.* Which begs the question: **What makes The Jesus Study different?**

Our initial answer is this:
Integrating film and video with Scripture

Primarily we focus on *The Chosen, but we also do other films such as The Life of Jesus* (John's Gospel), *RISEN,* and *Paul: Apostle of Christ*—each with the underlying Scriptures crafted into a ten-week experience. To that jumping-off point we add three additional qualities:

Jesus-centeredness

Personal growth through an evangelizing discipleship focus

Inductive, mark-it-up study

Those foundational traits are expanded into *twelve substantial distinctives* common to Jesus Studies. This distinguishing blend makes for a unique Bible study and God-encountering experience.

Twelve Distinctives of Jesus Studies

1. *Designed to be Jesus-centered* in the personal study, discussion and the "at home," quiet time experience.

2. *Intentionally includes an evangelizing discipleship focus* as a dual priority for personal and ministry growth among members.

3. *Combines film with complementary Scripture* passages along with *worship and teaching videos* to include visual elements of learning.

4. *Offers a skeptic- and seeker-friendly environment* to talk about Jesus among friends and colleagues in a ten-week time frame.

5. *Encourages food inclusion at each gathering* to facilitate connection among group members in a relaxed environment.

6. *Forms a core group that prays and prepares* to lead the various aspects of the group process and to spearhead outreach efforts.

7. *Embeds all Old and New Testament texts* into the guides for ready reference, especially for those unfamiliar with the Bible.

8. *Uses a four-colored BIC pen to mark up the texts* which employs an inductive mindset for observing, interpreting, and applying Scripture.

9. *Ends with a fun and memorable (paper) T-Shirt Design* which summarizes and crystallizes the learning process.

10. *Incorporates Drive it Home and Video Insights sections* after the study for additional, "at home," video learning opportunities.

11. *Grows Jesus-followers into group leaders* with dialogical facilitating skills and both a discipleship and evangelistic framework for ministry.

12. *Encourages leaders to equip others to lead new studies* within their own circles of influence—friends, family, and coworkers.

Take our No-Cost Bible Study 2.0
Orientation Session or Leadership Course

The Jesus Study is a 2.0 "evangelizing discipleship" experience. Again, what does this mean? *In a nutshell we combine film with Mark-It-Up Scripture study and invite our non-church friends to join us.* To help you excel at doing this, we'd like to have you join us on Zoom… OR…

We could also arrange to travel and meet up with you and your leadership team. We are serious about training and will work out what we can to assure you are equipped. Such help will give you a strong running start to your efforts.

How to Lead and Promote Your Group

Though years in the making, *The Jesus Study* formally came together on May 28, 2021, in a Zoom call led by Bill Syrios with some gifted Bible study leaders. Get in on that call and learn to lead in the process: tinyurl.com/lead-your-group

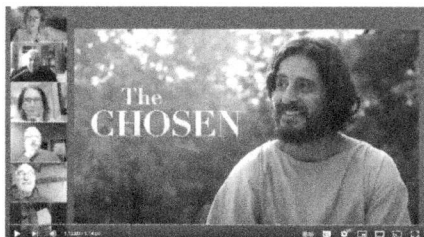

Let's do this thing!

Those Zoom calls continued, led by Bill with new-found colleagues. This next recorded call focuses an on effective means of promoting your group to new people: tinyurl.com/intro-your-group.

Our Mission: What We're About

The Jesus Study combines film depiction with Scripture in a welcoming and interactive experience for all: observers... skeptics... learners... seekers... followers, who WATCH > DISCOVER > RELATE together the Most Audacious Story ever told.

Our Executive Leadership Team: What We Do

We work with leaders, to help them create a friendly place to watch > discover > relate.

Back to Front, Left to Right:

Dave Hawkins, Tori Foss
and Dietrich Gruen
Bill & Teresa Syrios and
Cathy & Don Baker

Our Invitation: Zoom with us–Start a Group–Join the Team

Do you have some loaves and fish to bring to this endeavor? We are looking for those who have seen "the Jesus difference" and are interested in exploring how to spread that difference around the world using The Jesus Study. If that sounds like you, please contact us.

Your Faith Journey:

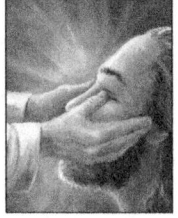

Made in the USA
Las Vegas, NV
06 February 2025

17671131R00115